English for
Telephoning

EXPRESS SERIES ■ ■ ■

David Gordon Smith

OXFORD

OXFORD
UNIVERSITY PRESS

Great Clarendon Street, Oxford OX2 6DP

Oxford University Press is a department of the University of Oxford.
It furthers the University's objective of excellence in research, scholarship,
and education by publishing worldwide in

Oxford New York

Auckland Cape Town Dar es Salaam Hong Kong Karachi
Kuala Lumpur Madrid Melbourne Mexico City Nairobi
New Delhi Shanghai Taipei Toronto

With offices in

Argentina Austria Brazil Chile Czech Republic France Greece
Guatemala Hungary Italy Japan Poland Portugal Singapore
South Korea Switzerland Thailand Turkey Ukraine Vietnam

OXFORD and OXFORD ENGLISH are registered trade marks of
Oxford University Press in the UK and in certain other countries

© Oxford University Press 2007

ISBN-13: 978 0 19 457928 5

Typeset by Oxford University Press
in Meta

Printed in Spain by Just Colour Graphics, S.L.

ACKNOWLEDGEMENTS
Illustrations by: Jaquie O'Neill
Photo credits: Oxford University Press, Classet
Cover images courtesy of: Corbis (main image/Kevin Do
Images (bottom left/Justin Pumfrey/Iconica), and Pun
(top left/Photodisc)

MultiROM

English for Telephoning is accompanied by a MultiROM which
has a number of features.

Interactive exercises to practise useful phrases, vocabulary,
and communication through your computer.

Listening extracts. These are in enhanced audio format that
can be played on a conventional CD-player or through the
audio player on your computer.

Useful documents including an A-Z wordlist in PDF format that
you can print out and refer to.

If you have any problems, please check the technical support
section of the readme file on the MultiROM.

Contents

About the book

In today's world there are very few jobs that do not involve the daily use of the telephone – and due to globalization, the language used on the telephone in business contexts is increasingly English. Even for people with a high level of English, speaking on the telephone presents a particular set of difficulties, for example sound quality. Not being able to see the body language of the person you are speaking to also makes telephone communication more problematic than a face-to-face conversation. However, by learning some of the conventions of the language of telephoning you can overcome some of these difficulties and develop your ability to hold efficient telephone conversations.

English for Telephoning offers you training in how to sequence a conversation and in strategies for communicating by telephone, as well as teaching typical expressions that will allow you to speak on the telephone successfully and with confidence.

English for Telephoning consists of six units that each deal with specific areas related to communicating by telephone. The book is structured so that the more basic skills are dealt with at the beginning of the book and it becomes progressively more advanced. However, the sequence is not fixed and the user can choose the units most relevant to their needs.

Each unit begins with a **Starter**, which consists of a quiz or a questionnaire that allows you to analyze your own use of the telephone. There are realistic listening exercises which offer practice in listening comprehension as well as presenting language and communication strategies. Throughout the units there are exercises that allow you to review your telephone English, learn new expressions and vocabulary, or to practise core grammatical structures. The role plays give you the opportunity to put all you have learnt into practice. At the end of each unit there are listening and reading activities designed to generate interesting conversations related to the theme of the unit. These are called **Output**. Finally, the book closes with a fun crossword to **Test yourself!** on all you have learnt over the previous six units.

The **MultiROM** contains all the **Listening extracts** from the book. These can be played through the audio player on your computer, or through a conventional CD-player. In order to give yourself extra listening practice, listen to it in your car. The **Interactive exercises** let you review your learning by doing **Useful phrases, Vocabulary, and Communication** exercises on your computer, this will be particularly valuable if you are using the book for self-study. There is also an **A-Z wordlist** with all the key words that appear in **English for Telephoning**. This includes a column of phonetics and a space for you to write the translations of the words in your own language.

In the appendices of **English for Telephoning** you will find the **Partner Files** for the role plays, the **Answer key** so that you can check your own answers if you are working alone. There are also **Transcripts** of the listening extracts and three pages of **Useful phrases and vocabulary**, which can be used as a handy reference when speaking on the telephone at work.

1 'Shall I put you through?'

Work with a partner. Ask him or her the questions below and make a note of the answers. Then tell the class what you found out.

1 How often do you make phone calls in English?

2 When was the last time you made or received a phone call in English? How was it?

3 Who do you normally speak English to on the phone? Are they native speakers or non-native speakers of English?

4 What do you find most difficult about telephoning in English?

5 Describe your worst experience with an English phone call.

AUDIO
2–4

1 **Three people are calling the company Micah Information Systems. Listen to the three dialogues and complete the table.**

	CALL 1	CALL 2	CALL 3
Who is calling?			
Who does he/she want to speak to?			
Does he/she get through? If not, why not?			
What will happen next?			

British English	American English
The line is engaged.	The line is busy.
mobile (phone)	cell (phone)

AUDIO

2-4

2 **Listen again and complete the sentences from the dialogues.**

1 Micah Information Systems. Sylvia _____ .

2 I'll _____ Mr Seide you _____ .

3 It's Karen Miller _____ .

4 I actually _____ to speak to Maria.

5 Just _____ on a moment while I make the

_____ .

6 I'm _____ Maria's line is _____ .

7 I'll try _____ later.

8 Let me just _____ a pen.

9 Nice to _____ from you.

10 I'm actually talking to someone on the other _____ .

Which sentences (1–10) can be used:

a to say who you are? *1, 3*

b to open a conversation politely? _____

c to say who you want to speak to? _____

d to put a caller through to another person? _____

e to say that somebody (or you) can't talk now? _____

f to say you will call again later? _____

g to take or leave a message? _____

3 **Match the halves to make questions from the dialogues.**

1	Could I speak	my mobile number?
2	Can I take	through to her?
3	Could you ask	have your number?
4	Could you tell me	back in ten minutes?
5	Does Mr Seide	your name again?
6	Is she there	a message?
7	Shall I put you	ask what it's about?
8	Can I just	at the moment?
9	Can I call you	to Jörg Seide, please?
10	Have you got	him to call me back?

Now match these answers to the questions. Sometimes more than one answer is possible.

a Certainly.

b Yes, he does.

c Sure, no problem.

d My name is John Ellis.

e Yes, I have.

f That would be great.

g Yes, she is.

h I'm afraid he's in a meeting.

i I need to ask her about the project meeting next week.

j Yes, please.

4 We can normally say the same thing in a more formal or less formal way.
Find pairs of expressions with the same meaning and complete the table.

~~Can I speak to Bob, please?~~ Certainly. ~~Could I speak to Bob, please?~~

Thanks. What's it about? Could you please hold? Hang on a moment.

Can I just ask what it's about? Shall I put you through to her? Sure.

Do you want to speak to her? Thank you.

MORE FORMAL	LESS FORMAL
Could I speak to Bob, please?	*Can I speak to Bob, please?*

5 There are different ways to give our names on the telephone. Match the sentences to the
explanations. (Careful: one sentence below is not used on the telephone!)

1 This is Gordon Wallis.
2 It's Gordon (Wallis) here.
3 Here is Gordon Wallis.
4 Gordon (Wallis) speaking.

a You say this when you answer the phone.
b You say this when you call a company and you
  don't know the person who answers the phone.
c You say this when you call someone you know.

USING FIRST NAMES

Whether we use first names or family names with people in English normally depends on the relationship
we have with them. Here are some tips.

- As a general rule, do what the other person does.
  So if the other person uses your first name, use
  their first name when you speak to them. One
  important exception: if the other person has a
  much higher status than you (for example if you
  are a secretary and they are a manager) then
  sometimes it's better to use their family name,
  even if they use your first name. It depends on
  the company culture.

- If it's the very first time you speak to a person,
  you should probably use their family name.
- If you've had contact with the person before
  (even if it was only on the phone), you can
  normally use first names.
- If the person is an important business contact,
  you should definitely try to use first names, if
  appropriate. It's a sign of a close working
  relationship.

AUDIO
2–4

6 Look at – or listen to – the three phone calls in exercise 1 again. Who uses first names,
and who uses family names? Why?

GIVING 'BAD' NEWS

It's very common for native speakers to use *I'm afraid* or *I'm sorry* when giving 'bad' news, for example when saying someone isn't available.

> **I'm afraid** Mr Seide is in a meeting.
> **I'm sorry, but** Mr Seide is in a meeting.

If you don't use *I'm afraid* or *I'm sorry*, the sentence sounds very direct and impolite to a native speaker.

The word *actually* is also often used to make a statement more polite. For example, it can be used:

- instead of saying the word **no**. A: *Does he have your phone number?* B: **Actually**, *I don't think he does.*
- when we change the subject (e.g. when we change from small talk to talking business). *Your holiday sounds fantastic. Listen, Sandra, I* **actually** *wanted to speak to Maria.*
- to say something which is inconvenient or annoying for the other person, in a polite way. *Can I call you back? I'm* **actually** *talking to someone else on the other line.*

Careful: *actually* is not the same as *current(ly)*!

7 **Rewrite the highlighted sentences below with *I'm afraid* or *actually*.**

1 I'm trying to get through to Jake Woodward. He asked me to call him this morning.
   I'm actually trying to get through ...
2 Marie Dupont. You're from France, aren't you? – No, I'm from Belgium.
3 Can I talk to Kevin Shields? – He's not here.
4 Would you like to leave a message? – No, I'll call back later.
5 Can I call you tomorrow? – I won't be in the office tomorrow.
6 Heather's line is engaged. Shall I tell her to call you back?

8 **Make excuses for why your boss doesn't want to come to the phone. Try to use *I'm afraid*, *I'm sorry*, or *actually* in each sentence. Remember that you don't always need to tell the truth when making an excuse!**

EXAMPLE

I'm afraid she's unavailable. She's actually in a meeting at the moment.

EXCUSES

having lunch
out of the office today/this afternoon
on a business trip
in a meeting
on another line

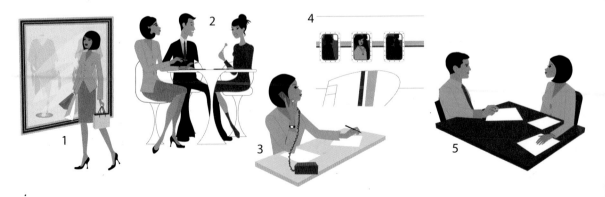

9 **Work with a partner to practise the dialogue below.**

A   **B**

Answer phone.   Say hello and make some small talk.

Respond.   Change subject and ask to speak to somebody.

Person is unavailable. Say why
and offer to take message.   Leave message.

Take message.   Say thank you and goodbye.

10 **Often when we telephone we have to deal with communication problems. Listen to the dialogues and match the problem to the call. Sometimes more than one answer is possible.**

AUDIO
5–12

	CALL
a The caller is speaking too quietly.	☐
b The person called didn't understand what the caller said.	*1*
c The person called wants the caller to say something again.	☐
d The caller is speaking too fast.	☐
e The caller has called someone by mistake.	☐
f The person called doesn't know how to write a word.	☐
g The phone itself is making a lot of noise.	☐
h The previous call was cut off and the caller has to call the other person back.	☐

Now complete the phrases from the dialogues with words from the list. Then listen again to check your answers.

slowly • up • cut • line • catch • spell • could • wrong

1 Sorry, I didn't _____ that.

2 Sorry, _____ you repeat that, please?

3 Sorry, can you speak _____ a bit, please?

4 Sorry, I think you have the _____ number.

5 Sorry, this is a really bad _____ .

6 Sorry, we got _____ off.

7 Sorry, could you _____ that for me, please?

8 Sorry, could you say that a bit more _____ , please?

11 Work with a partner to make two phone calls. Look at the Useful Phrases below before you read your role card in the Partner Files.

PARTNER FILES ➤ Partner A File 01, p. 48
Partner B File 01, p. 50

USEFUL PHRASES

Giving your name
Gail Jones speaking.
This is Robert Smith from ABC Enterprises.
Hello, Jane. It's Elena Gonzalez here.

Getting through to the right person
Could/Can I speak to Mark, please?
I'd like to speak to Ellen Baker, please.
I actually wanted to speak to Pat.
Is Pascal there at the moment?

Making the connection
Shall I put you through to him/her?
Can I just ask what it's about?
Could you please hold?
Just hang on a moment while I make the connection.

When the person isn't available
I'm afraid his/her line is engaged.
I'm afraid Pat isn't available at the moment.
I'm afraid she is in a meeting.
Can I take a message?
Would you like to call back later?

---

12 Complete the crossword, then rearrange the letters in the squares below to find the mystery word.

The mystery word is ☐ ☐ ☐ ☐ ☐ ☐ ☐ ☐ ☐

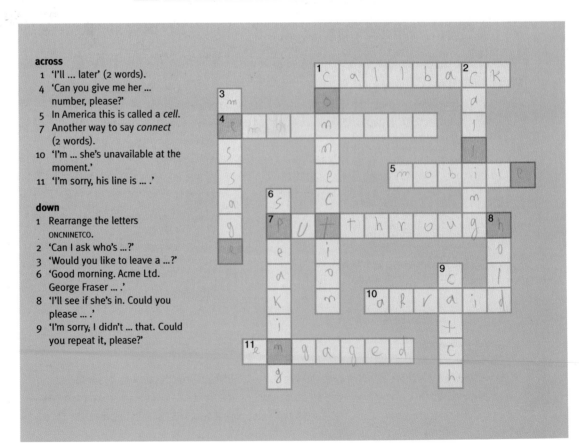

across
1 'I'll ... later' (2 words).
4 'Can you give me her ... number, please?'
5 In America this is called a *cell*.
7 Another way to say *connect* (2 words).
10 'I'm ... she's unavailable at the moment.'
11 'I'm sorry, his line is ... .'

down
1 Rearrange the letters ONCNINETCO.
2 'Can I ask who's ...?'
3 'Would you like to leave a ...?'
6 'Good morning. Acme Ltd. George Fraser ... .'
8 'I'll see if she's in. Could you please ... .'
9 'I'm sorry, I didn't ... that. Could you repeat it, please?'

13 **Put these sentences from the unit into the right order.**

1 speaking Kyoko Ito.

2 Juan Suarez is this. to speak I can please Ms Sanders.

3 call back I'll later.

4 office in Brenda today isn't the.

5 number do have my you mobile?

6 today I'm Mr Chang in isn't office afraid the.

7 called him I'll that you tell.

OUTPUT **What advice would you give to someone to help them telephone successfully? Work with a partner to make a list of tips. Then read the article and discuss the questions.**

Successful telephoning

Phone calls can often be challenging in your own language, but when you're speaking a foreign language they are even more difficult. There's no body language to help you, the audio quality is not always perfect, and there is more time pressure than in a face-to-face conversation. Below are some tips to make telephoning in English less stressful.

1 If you have to make a difficult phone call, spend a few minutes preparing first. Think about what you want from the phone call. What might the other person say? Make notes of English phrases you can use during the call.

2 Try to relax. Make sure you have enough time for the call, and don't hurry. It's better to have a successful ten-minute call than an unsuccessful five-minute call.

3 Sometimes receiving an unexpected call can be very stressful. To give yourself some time to prepare for the call, you might want to tell a 'white lie' (*I'm sorry, I'm actually in a meeting right now. Can I call you back in ten minutes?*) and call back when you feel more confident.

4 It's important to make a little small talk with the other person before you talk business, but don't spend too long chatting. Get to the point of the call quickly. If you're talking to a native English speaker, listen for words like *well*, *so*, and *anyway* – these are signals that it's time to talk business.

5 Speak more slowly and at a lower pitch than you would during a face-to-face conversation. It makes you sound confident, helps the other person to understand you, and calms you down if you are nervous.

6 Don't be afraid to ask a caller to repeat something (*I'm sorry, I still didn't catch that. Could you say it again more slowly?*). It's better for the caller to repeat a piece of information five times than for you to write down the wrong information.

7 Smile! Although it sounds strange, the other person can hear if you are smiling – it makes your voice sound friendlier.

OVER TO YOU

What is the thing you find most difficult on the telephone? How could you make it easier?

Can you think of five things you could do to improve your telephoning skills in English? For example, record English calls and listen to them with your English teacher, or telephone an English-speaking friend for practice.

2 'Could you spell that for me?'

How good are you at giving information over the phone? Do this quiz on numbers and symbols. Compare your answers with a partner's, then check your answers in the key.

1 How do you say these numbers in English?

(a) 647
(b) 9,235
(c) 1,574,389
(d) 1.955
(e) €15.40
(f) 0049 30 29706634

I can think of at least 15 reasons why I should fire you!

Sorry – did you say 15 or 50?

2 What does a comma (,) show in an English number? And a point (.)?

3 What are these symbols called in English?

(a) (b) (c) (d)
bob_jones@abc-company.com

(e) / _____
(f) \ _____
(g) # _____
(h) * _____
(i) (_____
(j)) _____

M-ROM

Refer to the *Numbers, dates, times, symbols* page of the MultiROM for more information about saying numbers and symbols in English.

AUDIO 13–14

1 Arno Maier works in a small import/export company in Hamburg. Listen to the two calls Arno makes and receives, and correct the mistakes in the notes.

relay switch
model RS 788 877

unit price:
1000 units = €1.65 1.56
2000 units = €11.39 1.49

Misha Oberemok
delivery address
Mitscevitch Ulittsa 6 Kovitch
97000 Kiev 79000
Fax no. (+380 44)
244 4240

AUDIO

13–14

2   **Listen to the dialogues again and complete the phrases below.**

Call 1

I have a question ____about____ [1] your relay switches. Are you the ____right____ [2] person to ask?

What ____was____ [3] your question?

Could you ____tell____ [4] me what the unit price would be for orders over a thousand units?

That was the RS 877, ____right____ [5]?

Sorry, I didn't ____catch____ [6] the second price.

Call 2

I'm ____calling____ [1] about the order you faxed us yesterday.

I just wanted to ____check____ [2] it.

Do you have a ____pen____ [3]?

Would you like me to ____spell____ [4] that for you?

Let me just ____read____ [5] that back to you.

Sorry, what was the post code ____again____ [6]?

HOW TO BE LESS DIRECT

Generally in English, the less direct a sentence is, the more polite it is. For example, we often use the past tense (*was, wanted*) instead of the present tense (*is, want*). The past tense is more polite, because it's less direct.

*What **was** your question?*
*I just **wanted** to check ...*
*I **wanted** to ask about ...*

Similarly, we often use *could* and *would* to make questions or statements less direct.

***Could** you tell me what the price **would be**?* (instead of ***Can** you tell me what the price **is**?*)
*What **would be** your preferred means of payment?* (instead of *What **is** your ...?*)

---

3   **Rewrite the sentences below to make them less direct as in the example.**

1   What is your question? __*What was your question?*_____

2   Can you tell me your name? _____

3   I just want to check the address. _____

4   What is your name again? _____

5   What do you want to know? _____

6   What is your charge for delivery? _____

7   How long does it take to send it? _____

8   I want to ask if you have time to meet tomorrow. _____

_____

ACTIVE LISTENING STRATEGIES

Active listening strategies can help you to communicate more effectively on the telephone.

When listening, say words like *right*, *uh huh*, *got you*, *yeah* every few seconds to show that you are paying attention. The other person feels more relaxed because it's clear that you are there and actively listening to them.

Check each piece of information that the other person gives you – even if you think you have understood everything perfectly, you might have actually misunderstood something the other person said.
You can do this by:

- Echoing, in other words by repeating what the other person said, to make sure you understood correctly:
  A *We can deliver on Tuesday.*
  B *Tuesday. Right.*

- Asking for clarification:
  A *Our address is 40 George Street.*
  B *Sorry, did you say 40 or 14?*

- Reading numbers and other important pieces of information back to the other person:
  A *My number is 2389 5354.*
  B *Let me just read that back to you. So that's 2389 5354.*

  You can also ask the other person to read a number back if they don't do it themselves:
  Can you just read that back to me?

4 **Complete these excerpts from a telephone conversation with words from the box.**

And your name was • Did you say • Let me just read that back to you. •
So that's • Sorry, was that • To Poland?

1 *Iwona*   Well, first of all, how long would it take to ship a consignment to Poland?

   George   _____[1]. I would say between a week and ten days by sea. We could also send a shipment via air freight, but that would naturally be more expensive.

   Iwona   _____[2] a week to ten days?

   George   Yes, that's right.

   •

2 *Iwona*   So that's 58 for Gdansk, then 61 3453.

   George   _____[3] 3453 or 2453?

   Iwona   It's 34 53.

   George   Right. _____[4] It's 00 48 5861 3453.

   Iwona   Yes, that's right.

   •

3 *George*   Great. _____[5] Iwona ...?

   Iwona   Jakubik. That's spelt J-A-K-U-B-I-K.

   George   _____[6] Iwona Jakubik.

   J-A-K-U-B-I-K. Got you.

5 **Check that you've understood. Ask about the highlighted information as in the example. More than one answer is possible each time.**

1   I would like to order 50 units. *Sorry, did you say 50 or 15 units? / OK, so that's 50 units.* _____

2   Our address is 98 King Street, Hull. _____

3   My phone number is 091 210 3885. _____

4   The meeting is on Thursday. _____

5   My name is Oliver Prentice. _____

6   The new price is €72.90. _____

6 **Do you know how to say the alphabet in English?**

Complete this table by putting the letters of the alphabet into the correct columns according to how you say them. For example, C /siː/ goes into the same column as B /biː/, because they have the same vowel sound. If a letter doesn't fit into an existing column, put it into a new column.

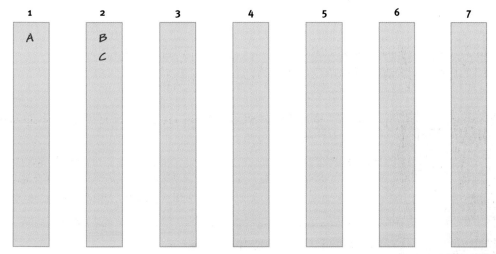

1	2	3	4	5	6	7
A	B					
	C					

SPELLING

Although there is an official English spelling alphabet (developed by NATO and used by the military and by radio operators), most English speakers do not know it. Instead, they use common words or personal names to spell words. For example, to spell NATO, an English speaker might say:

That's N for Neil, A for apple, T for Thomas, O for orange.

Notice that in English we say *N **for** Neil* or *N **as in** Neil (AE)*, not ~~N like Neil~~.

---

7 **Work with a partner to practise spelling. You'll find a list of place names in your file. Spell the names in your list for your partner and write down the names your partner spells for you.**

PARTNER FILES ➤ Partner A   File 02, p. 48
Partner B   File 02, p. 50

8 Write the email and website addresses in words as in the examples.

1 alan.thompson@hotmail.com   *Alan dot Thompson at hotmail dot com*

2 *www.gopher-systems.com   *w w w dot gopher hyphen systems dot com*

3 kevin.stevens@afg-consulting.ca _____

4 margaret_peterson@zebra.it _____

5 www.rent-a-car.com _____

6 (your email address) _____

7 (your company website address) _____

* Remember that the letter *w* is pronounced *double you* in English.
* Some people say *dash* instead of *hyphen*. However we don't normally say *minus* in email addresses.

Now practise reading the addresses out loud.

get info (that's one word) at high dash five dot org dot uk

getinfo@high-five.org.uk

9 Find ten sentences from this unit. Start at the numbered word, then move one square at a time (left, right, up, or down).

1 Do	2 Let	me	just	check	that.	person	to	ask?	3 I'm
you	have	that	read	just	4 Are	right	the	about	calling
5 What	a	back	6 Let	me	you	the	order	you	7 Would
would	pen?	to	back	to	you?	8 What	you	like	me
you	like	you.	get	give	me	was	faxed	us	to
know?	to	that	and	just	your	your	question?	yesterday.	spell
9 Can	I	check	10 Can	you	phone	number?	you?	for	that

Use the sentences you found above to complete the two dialogues. Sometimes more than one answer is possible.

1 *Kevin*   Mahoney Engineering. Kevin speaking.

Fiona   Hello Kevin. This is Fiona from ALP Supplies. _____ ^A.

I have a question about one of the items. _____ ^B.

Kevin   I'm not sure, but I'll do my best! _____ ^C.

Fiona   Well, the item number HG 892375 is out of stock at the moment, and I wanted to ask if the HG 892376 would be okay instead? It's almost the same model.

Kevin   Oh Fiona, I'm not totally sure. _____ ^D.

Fiona   Sure, no problem.

Kevin   Great. _____ ^E.

Fiona	Of course. It's 0248 294 413.
Kevin	Right. _____ ^F. Your number is 0248 294 413.
Fiona	That's right.
Kevin	Okay Fiona, I'll talk to my boss and I'll call you back later today.
Fiona	Great. Bye now.
Kevin	Bye.

....

2	*Kathy*	Voland Information Services. Kathy speaking.
	Paul	Hi Kathy. It's Paul here. I just have a quick question about the software you installed for us last week.
	Kathy	Oh, hi Paul. Nice to hear from you._____ ^G.
	Paul	Well, I'm afraid we've lost the dummy user name for the test set-up. Can you give it to us again?
	Kathy	Sure. No problem. _____ ^H.
	Paul	Yes, I do. Fire away.
	Kathy	OK. The user name is 'Joe.Bloggs'. _____ ^I.
	Paul	Yes please.
	Kathy	OK. It's J-O-E dot B-L-O-G-G-S.
	Paul	_____ ^J. The user name is 'Joe.Bloggs', spelt J-O-E dot B-L-O-G-G-S.
	Kathy	That's right.
	Paul	Well, thanks very much Kathy.
	Kathy	You're welcome. Bye now.

10   Work with a partner to make two phone calls. Look at the Useful Phrases below before you read your information in the Partner Files.

> **PARTNER FILES** ➤ Partner A   File 03, p. 48
> Partner B   File 03, p. 50

USEFUL PHRASES

Opening the call	**Exchanging information**	**Checking information**
I'm calling about ...	What was your question?	Would you like me to spell that for you?
I have a question about ...	What would you like to know?	Did you say ...?
I wanted to ask about ...	Could you tell me ...?	Sorry, I didn't catch that.
Are you the right person to ask?		Let me just read that back to you.
		Let me just check that.

---

11   Put these sentences from the unit into the right order.

1   have you pen do a?
2   six order A is elephant for Venice two zero E V the for number for apple (AEV 026).
3   D for Bob that B was or David for?
4   address D Tom at his hyphen dot Baker E email is Martins (tom-baker@martins.de).
5   didn't that sorry I catch. thirteen did thirty say or you?

Read the article and discuss the questions.

Get active with your listening

Imagine you are calling an important business contact. The person says he is in a hurry and only has five minutes for the call. While you are talking, you hear him typing on his computer keyboard, and he continually interrupts you while you are trying to talk. How would you feel?

The above description is an example of a bad listener. Everyone learns at school how to read and write, but normally we are never taught how to listen. However, effective listening is one of the most important communication skills.

Yes, of course I'm listening.

Here are some things you can do to improve your active listening skills.

1 Remove distractions. Make sure the place where you are telephoning isn't too hot, too cold, too noisy or too uncomfortable.

2 When you're on the phone, don't type, tidy your desk or organize your papers. The noises you make will tell your partner that you're not listening.

3 Forget about your own problems and tasks while talking to your partner. You can't concentrate on what someone else is saying if you are thinking about your 'to do' list.

4 Regularly summarize what your conversation partner has told you, to show that you are listening ('So what you mean is …', 'If I understood you correctly, you want to …'). This can also help your partner to move forward in the conversation.

5 Be honest with your partner. If you weren't paying attention to what they said, or if their English is too difficult, tell them and ask them to repeat what they said ('Sorry, could you say that again?', 'I'm sorry, but I'm finding you difficult to understand. Could you maybe try to talk in simpler English, please?').

6 Wait until the other person has stopped talking before you decide what to say next. If you are constantly thinking about your response, you won't be able to concentrate on what they are saying. Use phrases like 'let me see', 'I see what you mean', or 'I just need to think for a moment' to give yourself time to think about what to say next.

7 Learn listening skills from other people. Pay attention to how other people (especially native speakers) show you that they are listening.

Are you a good listener? Why / Why not?

How could you improve your own listening skills?

Can you think of people you know who are good/bad listeners? How do you feel when you speak to them?

'Let me get back to you on that.'

STARTER

Look at these voicemail greetings from four different companies.
Which is the best in your opinion? Why?

*1 Hello. You've reached
Yo-Yo Design.
Leave a message.*

*2 You've reached Hudson Engineering.
Unfortunately no one is available to take
your call at the moment. You can call us
back during normal office hours. Leave
a message after the tone or send us
a fax on 0177 813 814 11. Thank you.*

*3 Hello. Fusion Financial Services,
Joel Parker speaking. There's no one
here at the moment, but you can leave
a message after the beep and we'll
call you back as soon as we can.*

*4 Hi, this is Cecilia's voicemail.
I'm out of the office until the 5th.
If it's urgent, please contact Jeff
Yuong on extension 439. Thanks.*

**Does your company or do you have a
voicemail greeting in English?
If so, what is it? If not, work with a
partner to write one.**

> **NOTE**
>
> Some people still say *answerphone or
> answering machine* for voicemail.

AUDIO

15–16

1 Listen and write down the messages.

> ☏ **MESSAGE**
> For Walter Jackson
> From

> ☏ **MESSAGE**
> For
> From

What is wrong with the second message? What would your reaction be if you received it?

AUDIO

15

2 Listen to the voicemail greeting and the first caller's message again and complete the phrases.

> You've _____ [1] Lessa Logistica. _____ [2] no
> one is _____ [3] to take your call at the moment.
> Please _____ [4] a message after the _____ [5].

_____ [6] is Walter Jackson _____ [7] for Valeria Giuliani.

Maybe you can _____ [8] back to me as soon as you've _____ [9] the date and time with everyone.

I think you have my number already, but here it is _____ [10], just in _____ [11].

Hope to speak to you _____ [12].

HOW TO STRUCTURE A MESSAGE

It's important to structure your message clearly when you speak on an answering machine.
Here is one way to do it.

- Say who you are and (if necessary) who you are leaving the message for. *Hello, this is … calling for …*
- Explain the message step by step. *I'm calling about … / I just wanted to confirm …*
- Say what action you would like the other person to take (if any). *Maybe you could get back to me … / Could you call me back …?*
- Make sure the other person knows how to contact you. *Here's my number … / You can reach me on …*

Don't forget to keep your message as short as possible and to talk slowly and clearly.

---

3 First call Walter Jackson back (message 1) and speak on his voicemail to confirm the date and time of the meeting. Then use your notes from exercise 1 to rewrite Seth Prescott's message (message 2).

4 Work with a partner to practise leaving messages.

PARTNER FILES ➤ Partner A   File 04, p. 48
Partner B   File 04, p. 50

AUDIO
17–18

5 Anke Schmidt works at JKL Consulting in Stuttgart. Listen to these two phone calls she receives and say in which call ...

a the caller gets through. ☐

b the caller leaves a message. ☐

c the caller gives his or her phone number. ☐

d Anke says she will ring back. ☐

e Anke says she will ask a colleague to ring back. ☐

Now listen again and write down the two messages.

CALL 1

CALL 2

AUDIO
17

6 Put these sentences from the first call into the right order. Then listen again to check.

1 afraid here I'm the isn't at moment Jonathan.

2 message like him leave would to a for you?

3 me pen get let a.

4 call Jonathan shall ask you back I to?

5 number he does your have?

6 gets I'll your make Jonathan message sure.

AUDIO
18

Now match the beginnings and endings of sentences from the second call. Then listen to check.

a I'm calling about

b You said that

c You told me

d Can I call you back later today

e Can you give it to me again

f I'll talk to Henry and

☐ Henry was too busy to join the team.

☐ just in case?

☐ as soon as I've had the chance to speak to him?

☐ that we could take Maria instead.

☐ the email you sent me yesterday.

☐ call you straight back.

REFERRING TO PREVIOUS COMMUNICATION

Normally when we are calling someone back, we need to refer to previous communication like a phone call or an email to explain why we are calling. This can involve reporting or summarizing what another person has said. When we do this, we normally put tenses one step back 'into the past', as in the examples below.

'Sorry, I'm too busy.'	You said that you **were** too busy.
'I **was** ill on Monday.'	She said that you **had been** ill on Monday.

If the situation we are talking about is still true or relevant, however, we don't always change the tense.

'I **can't** come to the meeting.'	He said that he **can't** come to the meeting. OR
	He said that he **couldn't** come to the meeting.
'I'**ll email** you asap.'	She said that she'**ll email** me asap. OR
	She said that she **would email** me asap.

We often use 'reporting verbs' like *ask, tell,* and *mention* when we are reporting what someone said. Look at the examples below and notice how the verbs are used.

'**Will** the 10th be OK for you?'	You **asked me if** the 10th would be OK for me.
'I **sent** the email on Monday.'	She **told me that** she had sent the email on Monday.
'I'**m thinking** about going.'	Jonathan **mentioned that** he was thinking about going.

7 Complete the sentences below as in the example.

1 'The quality is too low.'

They said *the quality was too low.* _____

2 'Maybe we can find another supplier.'

She told me _____

3 'It will be difficult to schedule a new meeting.'

He said _____

4 'Can you deliver earlier?'

They asked _____

5 'We hired two new employees.'

You mentioned _____

6 'I'm going to the UK in June.'

He told me _____

8 Complete the sentences using the prepositions from the box.

about • after • at • for • in • on • to • until

1 Unfortunately no one is available to take your call _____ the moment.

2 Please leave a message _____ the beep or send us a fax _____ 042 823 4421.

3 This is Adam Gray calling _____ Stefanie Renner.

4 I'm calling _____ the email you sent me yesterday.

5 Maybe you can get back _____ me.

6 I'll be _____ the office _____ 5 p.m. today if you want to call me.

9 **Use one word or phrase from each column as in the example to make eight sentences for dealing with messages.**

Can I	afraid	she	again just in case?
Can you	call	the email	back later today?
Could	calling about	you	for her?
Would you like	you get back	to me	gets your message.
I'm	please give me	your number	have my number already.
I'm	to leave	you	isn't here at the moment.
I'll	make sure	a message	on this asap, please?
I	think	she	you sent me yesterday.

a Can _I call you back later today?_ _____

b Can you _____

c Could _____

d Would you like _____

e I'm _____

f I'm _____

g I'll _____

h I _____

Now use the sentences above to complete the dialogue extracts below.

A Sorry, I'm really busy at the moment. _Can I call you back later today?_ [1]

B Sure, no problem. I'll be in the office all afternoon.

A _____ [2]
Is that right?

B Erm ... let me check. Hold on a second ... Yes, I have it here. 879 234 89.
Is that right?

A Yes, that's right.

A   I'm sorry, Martina isn't here at the moment. _____

_____ 3

B   Yes please. I'd like to know the date of the next project meeting.

A   OK. _____ 4

A   It might be easier if she calls me. I'll be in the office until 3 pm today.

B   OK. I think we've got your contact details, but _____

_____ 5

A   Of course. It's 011 324 893 25.

A   Can I speak to Beate Schulze, please?

B   Oh, _____ 6 Can I

take a message?

Hi Patrice. This is Roland. _____ 7

There seems to be a problem with the schedule. _____

_____ 8

10   **Work with a partner to make two phone calls. Look at the Useful Phrases below before you look at your role card in the Partner Files.**

PARTNER FILES ➤ Partner A   File 05, p. 49
Partner B   File 05, p. 51

USEFUL PHRASES

Taking a message	**Leaving a message**
I'm afraid [name] isn't here at the moment.	This is [name]. I'm calling about …
Would you like to leave a message for her/him?	[name] asked me to call her/him (back).
Let me just check (that) I've got that right.	I just wanted to check/confirm/ask if …
Shall I tell [name] to call you back?	Could you ask her/him to call me back?
Does [name] have your number?	I'll be in the office today until …
I'll make sure [name] gets your message.	
I'll tell him/let him know that you called.	

11   **Put these sentences from the unit in the right order.**

1   544 332 64 reach you me can on.

2   for message her leave would to like you a?

3   call Eileen her asked to back me.

4   Mary Lamb is this. meeting calling about the I'm.

5   already sent he the told letter me had that he.

OUTPUT   **Do you love voicemail or hate it? Complete this survey to find out if you are message mad or if messages drive you mad!**

1   **What's your opinion of voicemail?**
a   I hate it. I only like talking to real people.
b   I don't like it much but I realize it can be useful.
c   I think voicemail is great. I couldn't live without it.

2   **What do you do when you call someone and get a message?**
a   Hang up and try again later.
b   Hang up, think about what to say, and phone back to leave the message.
c   Say what I need to say.

3   **How do you feel about leaving messages in English?**
a   I feel self-conscious in my own language, so I would never leave a message in English.
b   Self-conscious and nervous, I always prepare first.
c   I like it. I know I won't get an unexpected question and I will have time to say what I have to say.

4   **When do you have your voicemail on?**
a   Never.
b   Only when I know someone I don't want to speak to is going to call.
c   Quite often, when I am busy, or out of the office.

Results
If you answered:
Mostly a's – You are definitely a voicemail hater. You should try to see the advantages of voicemail, it can be very useful.

Mostly b's – You are comfortable with voicemail but you would really rather speak to the person you called.
Mostly c's – You are a voicemail lover. Maybe you love it too much. Do you prefer talking to machines than to people?

OVER TO YOU

What do you think are the advantages and disadvantages of using voicemail at work?
Do you ever play 'telephone tag' with business contacts? (You call them and leave a message, they call you back and leave a message etc.)
What tips can you think of for using voicemail effectively?

4 'When would suit you?'

STARTER

How well can you talk about times and dates in English? Try this quiz and compare your answers with a partner's. Then check your answers in the key.

1 **Which of the time expressions are not possible in English?**
   a   2 p.m.
   b   2 o'clock p.m.
   c   2 p.m. in the afternoon
   d   2 o'clock in the afternoon

2 **How do you say the following times in English?**
   a   *6:30*
   b   *10:15*
   c   *3:45*
   d   *0:00*
   e   *12:00*

3 **What does the date 01.02.06 mean to**
   a   an American person?
   b   a British person?

4 **Here are some ways to say the date 28 May 2005. Which are not possible in English?**
   a   the twenty-eighth of May, two thousand and five
   b   the twenty-eighth of May, two thousand five
   c   May twenty-eighth, two thousand and five
   d   the twenty-eighth May, two thousand and five
   e   the twenty-eight of May, two thousand and five

M-ROM

If you had trouble with this quiz, then refer to the *Numbers, dates, times, symbols* page of the MultiROM.

AUDIO
19

1 Simon Mellor works at London Bank in Frankfurt. Look at his diary for next week, then listen and write in the appointment that he makes.

British English	American English
diary	planner
mobile (phone)	cell (phone)
half (past) two	half past two

Monday

Tuesday
9–5 KPMG meeting

Wednesday

Thursday *4 pm telephone conference with US office*

Friday

Saturday

Sunday

2 **Listen again and complete the table with suitable phrases from the dialogue.**

SUGGESTING A MEETING OR AN APPOINTMENT	SAYING IF A TIME IS CONVENIENT OR NOT
I was wondering if you might have time to meet me while I'm in town.	

ASKING ABOUT OR SUGGESTING A TIME TO MEET	

	CONFIRMING AN ARRANGEMENT

Now add these useful phrases to the table above.

> Could we schedule a meeting for next month?

> Yes, I'm free then.

> OK, so that's 2 p.m. in the conference room.

> What about Thursday?

> Where would be the best place to meet?

> Do you have time to meet tomorrow?

3 **Use phrases from your table to practise a dialogue with a partner.**

A	B
Answer the phone.	Suggest a meeting and a time to meet.
Time is inconvenient. Suggest another time.	Time is inconvenient. Suggest another time.
Agree. Suggest a place to meet.	Agree and confirm the details.
Say goodbye.	

TALKING ABOUT ARRANGEMENTS

We usually use the present continuous with a future time expression to talk about arrangements.

*I'm flying in on **Monday morning**.*
*And then I'm **having dinner** with my client **in the evening**.*

AUDIO
20

4 **One of Alexa's clients in Frankfurt calls Hilary, Alexa's personal assistant. Look at the extract from Alexa's diary below and use the verbs in the box to complete the dialogue. Then listen to check your answer.**

> meet • come • have • fly • meet • come • have

	Monday	Tuesday	Wednesday
7am			
8am	8.10 fly to Frankfurt		
9am			
10am			meeting with Simon
11am			
12am	meeting with Yves Gainsbourg		
1pm		lunch with James Copeland	
2pm			meeting with Helmut Fischer
3pm			
4pm			
5pm			
6pm			6.45 fly to London
7pm	dinner with George (check)	dinner with Claire	
8pm			
9pm			
10pm			

Hilary JPL Consulting. Hilary Wilkins speaking.

Anna Hello Hilary. This is Anna Roth from Frankfurt. Is Alexa there?

Hilary I'm afraid she isn't. Can I help at all?

Anna Well, a colleague told me that Alexa _is coming_ [1] to Frankfurt next week. I'd like to see her while she's here, if she has time.

Hilary Okay. Well, let me look at her schedule and we'll figure something out. When would suit you best?

Anna I'm pretty flexible. Maybe you can tell me when she's free?

Hilary Let me see. Okay, so she _____ [2] to Frankfurt first thing on Monday morning. Then she _____ [3] a client at 12. In the evening she _____ [4] dinner with a friend.

Anna Hmm. Sounds like she's quite busy. What about Tuesday?

Hilary Well, she's free on Tuesday morning. But then she _____ [5] lunch with a colleague at 1 and she _____ [6] someone in the evening.

Anna Okay. And Wednesday?

Hilary That's pretty full. She has a couple of meetings during the day then she __coming__ [7] back to London in the evening.

Anna Okay. Well, maybe you can pencil me in on Tuesday morning. Say, 10 o'clock?

Hilary	10 o'clock on Tuesday. Okay, I'll double-check that with Alexa and send you a quick email to confirm the meeting.
Anna	Wonderful. Thanks for your help.
Hilary	You're welcome. Bye now.

Now work with a partner and ask each other about your appointments for this week or next week.

5 Use *in, on, at,* or *Ø* (= no preposition) to complete the time expressions.

1 _on_ Monday

2 _Ø_ tomorrow

3 ____ the morning

4 ____ Friday morning

5 ____ yesterday evening

6 ____ last night

7 ____ next week

8 ____ March 17th

9 ____ the weekend

10 ____ Christmas

11 _at_ 10 o'clock

12 _at_ midnight

13 _in_ March

14 _in_ 1990

15 _in_ the evening

SMALL TALK

Normally when we call someone we know, we make a little bit of small talk before we start talking business.
Here are some typical telephone small talk questions.

> *How are things in* [name of town] / *at* [name of firm]*?*
> *Are things busy with you?*
> *What have you been up to?* (=*What have you been doing recently?*)
> *How is the weather there?*
> *How was your holiday / your trip to* [name of place]*?*
> *How is* [name of husband/wife/partner] / *are the kids?*

Normally we mark the change from small talk to business with a signal word like *listen* or *anyway*, possibly followed by the name of the person we are talking to.

> **Listen** *Frank, I was* **actually** *calling about …*
> **Anyway** *Uta, I* **actually** *wanted to ask you if …*

---

6 Match the small talk questions to the answers.

1 How are things in Paris?

2 How's the weather in Glasgow?

3 How was your holiday in Spain?

4 How are the kids?

5 What have you been up to?

6 Are things busy with you?

7 How did the conference go?

a Nothing much, apart from work, to be honest. It's been really hectic here.

b Very well, thanks. The oldest one has just started school.

c Wet, as usual!

d It's not too bad, actually. But last month was a nightmare.

e Very nice. We had a great time.

f Great, I made lots of contacts.

g Oh, you know what it's like. Same old thing as always.

7 Work with a partner. First write down three 'small talk' questions (try to make them relevant to the other person). Then follow the steps below to make a phone call. Remember to use signal words like *so* and *well* to show when you want to move from one stage of the conversation to the next.

A

Answer the phone.

Respond. Ask small talk question.

Respond. Ask follow-up question (if appropriate).

B

Say hello. Say your name.

Respond. Ask small talk question.

Respond. Start talking about business.

AUDIO
21

8 It's now Monday morning and Alexa is calling Simon's personal assistant, Thorsten Hofmeister. Tick the sentences you hear.

1 I'm afraid something has come up. ☐
2 I'm afraid I have to reschedule our appointment. ☐
3 One of my clients has cancelled our appointment ... ☐
4 One of my clients has brought forward our appointment ... ☐
5 So I wanted to ask Simon if we could meet a bit earlier ... ☑
6 So I wanted to ask Simon if we could postpone our meeting ... ☐
7 Just let me know if there are any more changes. ☐
8 Just give me a call if there are any more changes. ☑

Simon – Alexa Johnston called

Listen again and complete Thorsten's message for Simon.

CHANGING AN ARRANGEMENT

If you want to change an arrangement, it's polite to give a concrete reason for doing so.

*I'm afraid **something has come up**. One of my clients has brought forward our appointment.*

The phrase *something has come up* means that something unexpected has happened and it's probably not something you can control.

Here are some ways to suggest or ask about changing an arrangement.

*So **I wanted to ask you if** we could meet **a bit** earlier in the morning.*
***I was wondering if** we could reschedule our appointment.*
***Could** we **possibly** postpone the presentation?*
***Would it be possible** to meet a bit later?*

9 **Complete the sentences below with words from the box.**

> bit • changed • delayed • lasted • missed • possible •
> possibly • postponed • wanted • wondering

1 I was _____ if we could meet on Friday instead. My client has _____ our schedule.

2 I _____ to ask if we could meet tomorrow instead of today. I've _____ my flight and I'm afraid I'm going to arrive very late.

3 Could we _____ cancel our appointment? My meeting _____ longer than I expected.

4 Could we meet a _____ later? I'm afraid my customer has _____ our meeting.

5 Would it be _____ to reschedule our meeting? My train has been _____ .

AUDIO
22

10 **It is now 8.50 a.m. on Tuesday morning and Alexa is calling Simon again. Listen to the conversation. Why is Alexa calling?**

Listen again and complete the phrases.

I'm actually still _____¹ for the train so I'm afraid I _____² be a few minutes late.

I should be there by 9.15 at the _____⁶, but I'll call you again if there are any more _____⁷.

Sorry, you're _____³ up a little. I didn't _____⁴ that last part.

I think I'm _____⁸ the connection. I'd _____⁹ go.

I'll see you when I _____⁵ you.

11 **Look at these phrases which are typical for mobile phone calls. Match the questions to the answers. Sometimes more than one answer is possible.**

1 Where are you?

2 Is this a good time to talk?

3 Have you got a couple of minutes?

4 Can you hear me?

5 Are you still there?

6 What was that beeping noise?

a You're breaking up a little. Would you like to try calling me again later?

b Yes, I am. I just lost the connection for a second.

c I'm on the train.

d I'm afraid I'm in a meeting at the moment. Can we talk later?

e Sure. What can I do for you?

f My battery's low – we might get cut off, I'm afraid.

g Not really, I'm afraid. Can I call you back later?

h I'm actually in the office. You can call me on my landline.

12 Complete the sentences with the correct form of the words in the box.

> appointment • arrangements • date • arrange • cancel •
> postpone • bring forward • date

1 What's the _____ today? Is it the 17th of March?

2 Unfortunately I have to _____ the meeting. I can't find a time when we can all meet.

3 I have a(n) _____ to see Ms Fraser.

4 They told me that the conference room is already booked for 2 p.m. and asked if we could _____ the meeting to 10 a.m. Is that OK for you?

5 The department secretary made all the _____ for my trip.

6 I have a(n) _____ with the new guy in purchasing tonight. We're going to see the new Tarantino movie.

7 It seems like a lot of people are ill or on holiday this week. Why don't we _____ the presentation until next week?

8 I'm calling to _____ a time to meet next week.

13 Work with a partner to make three phone calls. Look at the Useful Phrases below before you look at your 'diary' and the instructions in the Partner Files.

PARTNER FILES ➡ Partner A   File 06, p. 49
Partner B   File 06, p. 51

> **USEFUL PHRASES**
>
> **Making an arrangement**
> I was wondering if you might have time to meet next
>   week.
> What day/When would suit you?
> Can we fix a meeting for Tuesday?
> How about Monday morning?
> Shall we say 9 o'clock at my office?
>
> **Changing an appointment**
> I'm calling about our appointment.
> I'm afraid something has come up.
> I wanted to ask you if we could postpone/bring forward
>   our meeting.
> Could we possibly reschedule/cancel our appointment?
>
> **Saying you will be late**
> I'm afraid my meeting has taken longer than I
>   expected.
> I might be a few minutes late.
> I should be there by 3.15 at the latest, but I'll
>   call you again if there are any more delays.

14 Put these sentences from the unit into the right order.

1 has something I'm up afraid come.

2 the appointment she MD an has with.

3 few a late might I be late minutes.

4 New York Saturday I'm to flying on.

5 all tied I'm up day.

6 free afternoon Wednesday should be I on.

OUTPUT

Have mobile phones made our lives easier or are they just annoying and unnecessary? Listen to the four speakers and match what they say to the pictures. Which opinion(s) do you agree with?

AUDIO

23–26

Listen again and complete the phrases.

Speaker 1
Mobile phones can be _____, but I don't like the fact that people can always _____ me.

Speaker 3
I hate mobile phones! I think they're one of the most annoying _____ ever. And people make so many pointless _____ now.

Speaker 2
Surely they can let their _____ pick up and then listen to any _____ later.

Speaker 4
Now I never need to worry about being late for an _____; if I'm stuck in traffic, I just call and let the person _____.

OVER TO YOU

What do you think should be the rules of mobile phone etiquette? Make a list of do's and don'ts and discuss it with the class.

5 'I'm very sorry about that.'

STARTER

What are your attitudes to complaints?
Make a cross on the scale to represent how much you agree (5 = I agree 100%) or disagree
(0 = I disagree 100%).

> We are sorry...,
> We apologize...,
> We regret that...,
> We're afraid that...,

		agree			disagree		

1 I never apologize for a mistake someone else makes. `5` `4` `3` `2` `1` `0`

2 You should always accept responsibility for a problem if a customer makes a complaint. `5` `4` `3` `2` `1` `0`

3 I don't like complaining. Normally I accept bad service without saying anything. `5` `4` `3` `2` `1` `0`

4 If someone calls me with a complaint, I try to listen carefully. `5` `4` `3` `2` `1` `0`

5 I always try to find a colleague who can solve the problem if I can't do it myself. `5` `4` `3` `2` `1` `0`

6 Some people just enjoy complaining. I don't think you have to take every complaint seriously. `5` `4` `3` `2` `1` `0`

7 Customer complaints can help us improve our service. `5` `4` `3` `2` `1` `0`

Discuss your answers with a partner.

AUDIO
27–30

1 **Listen to the four short extracts from phone calls. In which call does the person called:**

a deal with the problem immediately? ☐   c connect the caller to the person responsible? ☐

b tell the caller to call another number? ☐   d promise to call the caller back? ☐

In which extract do you hear the following phrases?

A Let me put you through to our accounts department. ☐

B You seem to have forgotten the attachment. ☐

C Unfortunately I can't put you through directly, but let me give you the number. ☐

D Can I check that and call you back? ☐

E I'll send you the file right away. ☐

F You actually need to speak to our technical support hotline. ☐

G There appears to be a mistake on the invoice you sent us. ☐

H Some of the components don't seem to work. ☐

AUDIO
31

2 Listen to the conversation and take notes. What is the problem and how will Reva deal with it?

After the call, Reva writes an email to his boss about the problem. Use your notes (and listen again if necessary) to complete the email.

File   Edit   View   Insert   Format   Tools   Table   Window   Help

100%   Read

Send   Options...   HTML

From: Reva Burgos   **To:** Paula Kilroy
CC: **Subject:** Delivery problem

Hi Paula,

Just to let you know, I got a call from Abby Dickson from Sykes Electronics today. She told me that there

was a problem with the latest _____ [1] we sent them. Apparently, some of the _____ [2]

we sent them contained the wrong _____ [3] model. (They ordered the _____ [4] sensor,

but we sent the _____ [5] model instead.)

I told Abby I would send her the correct units by _____ [6] delivery with _____ [7] Logistics.

The logistics company will _____ [8] the other units up when they deliver the correct units.

Best wishes,
Reva

AUDIO
31

3 Listen again and find the missing words.

1   There _____ to be a small problem with your latest consignment.

2   Oh dear. I'm _____ to hear that.

3   What's the problem _____ ?

4   I'll _____ on to this problem immediately.   *sorte*

5   Well, _____ is what I'm going to do.

6   Thanks for _____ that out, Reva.

7   Again, I'm really sorry about the _____ .

8   I'll _____ make sure it doesn't happen again.

Now decide which of the sentences above you can use to do the following. Sometimes more than one answer is possible.

describe a problem *1*   apologize *7, 8, 2*
clarify what the problem is *1, 3*   say how you will solve the problem *5, 4*

COMPLAINING

Normally we explain the context before we explain our complaint in detail.

I'm calling / I have a question about the invoice you sent us.

In addition to *I'm afraid* and *unfortunately*, we often use verbs like *seem* and *appear* to describe the problem. These verbs make the complaint sound less aggressive and allow the possibility that we might be wrong.

***I'm afraid** there's a slight problem with the goods you sent us.*
***Unfortunately** it **seems** we haven't received the shipment.*
*It **seems** you forgot the attachment OR You **seem** to have forgotten the attachment.*
*There **appears** to be a small problem with your latest consignment.*

Rewrite these sentences to make them more polite. Use the words in bracket as in the example.

4 1 The parts you sent us don't work. (seem)   *The parts you sent us don't seem to work.*

2 You delivered the consignment to the wrong address. (unfortunately)

3 The total on the bill is wrong. (appears)

4 We have a problem with the equipment you sold us. (afraid/slight)

5 You sent us the wrong model. (seem)

6 You gave us the incorrect information. (unfortunately)

APOLOGIZING

There are different phrases you can use to apologize, for example:

I'm sorry about …
I'd like to apologize for … (more formal)
Please accept my / our apologies for … (very formal)

You can use words like *really*, *very*, and *extremely* or the expression *I have to say* to make an apology stronger.

*I'm **very** / **extremely** sorry about this.*
***I have to say** I'm **really** very sorry about this.*

If the mistake really is your (or your company's) fault, you can admit this by saying:

That's entirely our fault.
There must have been a mix-up.

SOLVING THE PROBLEM

Customers also appreciate it if you take responsibility for solving the problem. Here we often use the *will* future when we promise to do something (often spontaneously).

***I'll** get on to that problem immediately.*
***I'll** make sure it gets sorted out straight away.*
***I'll** personally make sure it doesn't happen again.*

If you don't want to make such a firm promise, you can use *should* instead.

*You **should** have them first thing tomorrow morning.*
*You **should** have it by Friday at the latest.*

5 Complete the two phone calls with words and phrases from the box.

> sorry again about the mix-up • I'll make sure that gets sorted out •
> it seems you sent us • there appears to be a mistake •
> please accept my apologies • I'm really sorry about • could you tell me

1 *Etta*   I'm calling about the business cards you did for us. _____

_____ [1] with the address.

Tania   Oh no. I'm very sorry to hear that. _____ [2] what the

mistake is exactly?

Etta   Well, you've printed the company address as one word, but it's actually two words.

Tania   _____ [3] for the mistake. That's entirely our fault.

_____ [4] straight away and we'll send you new

cards as soon as we can.

Etta   That sounds good. Thanks for your help.

•••

2 *Eric*   This is Eric Kessler from Fatima Networks. I'm calling about the software release you sent us

yesterday.

Basil   Uh huh. Is everything okay with it?

Eric   Actually, no. _____ [5] the old version. The disk has

version 2.2 on it, not 2.3.

Basil   Oh dear. _____ [6] that. I'll send you a new disk straight

away. You should get it first thing tomorrow.

Eric   That sounds good, thanks. I'll probably call you again when it arrives.

Basil   Do that. And _____ [7].

Eric   No problem.

Which conversation is more formal, and which is more informal?

6 Complete the sentences 1–5 with *'ll* and the verbs in the box.

> deliver • give • have • make sure • send

1 I *'ll send* _____ you the document straight away.

2 Don't worry. You _____ the goods by lunchtime tomorrow.

3 I _____ personally _____ it doesn't happen again.

4 We _____ you ten units free, by way of compensation.

5 The package is on its way. They _____ it by 5 p.m. today.

7 **Work with a partner to practise the following dialogue.**

A

B

Say you have a problem. → Ask what the problem is.

Explain the problem. → Admit responsibility and apologize.
Say what you will do to solve the problem.

Thank your partner. → Apologize again and say goodbye.

AUDIO

32

8 **Listen to the call to a technical support hotline and make notes to complete the form.**

Nexus Retail Systems	Technical Support
Call record	
1 Name of caller	
2 Company	
3 Description of problem	
4 Action taken	

AUDIO

32

9 **Listen to the call again and complete the phrases.**

1 Are you the _____ person to talk to?

2 Could you explain the problem in more _____ ?

3 I'm going to need some more _____ to solve the problem.

4 In that _____ , it must be the ink cartridge.

5 If you have any _____ just give me a _____ .

6 My name's Anja Schneider, but you can speak to _____ of our operatives here on the hotline.

10 **Work with a partner to make two phone calls. Look at the Useful Phrases below before you read your role card in the Partner Files.**

PARTNER FILES → Partner A   File 07, p. 49
Partner B   File 07, p. 51

USEFUL PHRASES

Explaining a problem
There seems/appears to be a problem with …
I'm afraid there's a problem with …
Unfortunately, you/we …

Explaining what you will do
This is what I'm going to do.
I'll send/revise/prepare …
I'll make sure it doesn't happen again.

Apologizing
I'm (really/very) sorry about that.
I have to say I'm extremely sorry about this.
Please accept my apologies.

11 Put these sentences from the unit into the right order.

1 small a there to with appears invoice problem be the.
2 be annoying must really that.
3 the thing consignment have tomorrow you should first.
4 for that thanks sorting out.
5 sure I'll again make it doesn't happen.

Read this article from a customer care magazine and answer the questions below.

DEALING WITH COMPLAINTS

Dealing well with complaints shows how important customer care is for your company. It shows that you listen to your customers, that you want to learn from your mistakes, and that you are continually trying to improve your services.

Below are some tips for dealing with complaints.

✓ TAKE EACH COMPLAINT SERIOUSLY

If you deal with a complaint in the wrong way, one unhappy customer may tell many more people about your poor service. On the other hand, if you deal with a complaint successfully, that customer will probably do business with you again. Remember that finding new customers is much more expensive than keeping current ones.

✓ LISTEN TO YOUR CUSTOMERS AND SHOW THEM YOU UNDERSTAND WHAT THEY ARE FEELING

Listen carefully to your callers and let them get rid of their anger or frustration. Try to see things from their point of view and make sure you show them that you understand their problem.

✓ ADMIT THAT A MISTAKE HAS BEEN MADE AND SAY SORRY

If the customer thinks something is a complaint, then it is, even if you think the problem is not important. If your company has really made a mistake, say so and apologize. Even if you think a mistake has not been made, show the customer that you understand the problem. Never tell the customer that the complaint is not important.

✓ ACCEPT PERSONAL RESPONSIBILITY

Even if you are not directly responsible for the mistake, it is not important for the customer whose fault it really is. You are the face of your organization and it is your responsibility to solve the problem. If you are not able to do so yourself, find the person who can. Make sure you support the customer until the right person can help.

✓ TAKE IMMEDIATE ACTION

Customers want their problems solved quickly. Acting fast shows customers that you take them and their problems seriously.

✓ OFFER COMPENSATION

If possible, try to compensate customers for a mistake, e.g. by giving a small discount. Often the fact that you are giving some kind of compensation is more important than the compensation itself.

✓ THANK THE CUSTOMER FOR MAKING THE COMPLAINT

This may sound illogical, but complaints are the best feedback you can get. They show how you can improve your service and make your customers more satisfied.

OVER TO YOU

Look back at the telephone calls in this unit. Do the people follow the advice given above? Does your company handle complaints well? How could it improve its complaints procedure? Think of a complaint you have made to another company. What was it? Was it dealt with?

6 'How does that sound?'

Work with a partner. Answer the questions first for yourself, then interview your partner and make a note of his or her answers.

	YOU	YOUR PARTNER
What kind of things do you make agreements about (e.g. prices, delivery times, conditions)?		
How often do you make agreements on the telephone?		
What problems do you have when discussing business on the telephone?		
Give an example of a successful (or an unsuccessful) agreement you have made on the telephone.		

AUDIO

33

1 **Carles Ferran works for a small company in Barcelona. He's calling a British supplier about a possible order and to get details about delivery times and prices. Listen and complete his notes.**

> Possible supplier: _____ ¹ Semiconductors
> Order _____ ² chips from them?
> We need chips by the _____ ³ of next month
> at the latest.
> Possible solution: introduce _____ ⁴ at the factory
> Problem: would be more expensive – _____ ⁵ to
> _____ ⁶ per cent?
> They will send _____ ⁷ by email, then we can talk
> again tomorrow.

AUDIO

33

2 **Match the sentence beginnings (1–6) and endings (a–f) to make sentences from the dialogue, then listen again to check.**

1 We need them
2 We really need them by then
3 If you weren't able to deliver by then,
4 However, if we introduced shift work at the factory,
5 Would you be prepared to pay more for the chips
6 Well, that sounds like

a if we're going to meet our project deadlines with our customer.
b then we would probably be able to manufacture the chips faster.
c in order to get them faster?
d by the middle of next month at the latest.
e it would be feasible.
f we would have to go to another supplier.

TALKING ABOUT POSSIBILITIES

When negotiating, it is common to use conditional forms to show that we are talking about possibilities. Read the examples.

Would you be prepared to pay more for the chips in order to get them faster?
If you weren't able to deliver by then, we **would have to** go to another supplier.
If we introduced shift work at the factory, **then we could manufacture** the chips faster.

Note that in *if*-sentences the simple past form of the verb (and not *would*) is used in the *if* part of the sentence.

*If we **introduced** shift work at the factory, then we could manufacture the chips faster.*
NOT: ~~If we would introduce ...~~

---

3 **Complete the conference call dialogue using the correct form of the words in brackets. Use *could* or *would* where appropriate as in the examples. Sometimes more than one answer is possible.**

A ... OK, so the next point is our British office. It's far too expensive and we urgently need to reduce our costs. Do any of you have ideas how we _could do_ ¹ (do) that?

B Well, if they _moved_ ² (move) into a smaller office, we _would save_ ³ (save) a lot of money on rent.

A Yes, but the move itself _____ ⁴ (cost) a lot of money. And it _____ _____ ⁵ (cause) a lot of disruptions to our business.

C What if we _____ ⁶ (reduce) the number of staff?

B That _____ ⁷ (cause) a lot of bad feeling among the rest of the staff. And paying people off _____ ⁸ (be) expensive.

C What about if we _____ ⁹ (give) the sales staff laptops and _____ ¹⁰ (ask) them to work from home? Most of the time they're travelling anyway. Then we _____ _____ ¹¹ (rent) out that office space to other people.

A That _____ ¹² (work). Let me think about it ...

HEDGES

Hedges (phrases which express doubt or make a statement sound less certain) are useful when making suggestions or tentatively agreeing to something. Native speakers of English often use words like *probably* and *might* or expressions like *I would say* and *I think I can provisionally say* when trying to reach an agreement.

> We could **probably** work with that.
> We **might** be able to work with that.
> **I would say** (it would be) between 5 to 10 per cent more expensive.
> **I think I can provisionally say** that we could work with that.

Note that the use of hedges is more common in British English than American English.

---

4 **Rewrite the sentences to make them more tentative. Using the words in brackets as in the example. Sometimes more than one answer is possible.**

1 We can give you a discount. (provisionally)

I think I can provisionally say that we will be able to give you a discount.

2 We can deliver by the end of the week. (might)

3 We can solve the problem. (would)

4 It will be difficult. (probably)

5 We can change the specifications of the product. (provisionally)

AUDIO
34

5 **Viktor Klein is calling a supplier to negotiate some prices. Listen and complete the email.**

Hi Alex

Just wanted to let you know that I've spoken to Francesca _____ ¹ at Hineman Pharmaceuticals about the saline solution order. You remember there was a problem with their _____ ², which was roughly _____ ³ higher than the competition. I asked if there was any chance of a _____ ⁴, and they said they can give us a _____ ⁵ reduction on orders over _____ ⁶ cases. I said I would check with you, then contact them if we want to place the order.

Let me know what you think.

Regards
Viktor

AUDIO
34

6 **Now listen again and complete the gaps with the words and phrases you hear.**

1 *Viktor* I'm calling because I wanted to _____¹ our conversation from yesterday.

Francesca That's right. You said you wanted to compare products and prices from different suppliers, _____²?

....

2 *Francesca* Wonderful. Shall I fax you the order form? We could …

Viktor Sorry, can I _____³ you there? There's actually one small problem.

....

3 *Francesca* Well yes, that _____⁴, but I think you'll find our quality is higher and …

Viktor Yes, yes, but can I just say _____⁵? I wanted to ask …

TURN-TAKING

It can be difficult on the telephone to know when to speak yourself and when to let your partner speak. Since you and the person you're talking to can't see each other, you have to use verbal instead of non-verbal techniques instead. Here are some suggestions.

- Ask questions and use question tags to show your partner that it's his or her turn to speak.

Questions	**Question tags**
How does that sound?	*You'll be in the office tomorrow, **won't you**?*
What do you think?	*You said you wanted to compare prices, **didn't you**?*
Is that OK?	

- Avoid silences – they can make the person you're talking to feel uncomfortable. (See the **Active listening strategies** box on page 14 for more advice.)
- Use a combination of the following phrases to interrupt politely if your partner won't let you speak.

Yes, yes, but	
Sure, but	*can I just say something?*
Sorry, (but)	*can I interrupt you there (for a second)?*
Of course, but	*can I stop you there?*

---

7 **Work with a partner. First, think of something that you have to discuss on the telephone (e.g. a price, a delivery date, a project deadline). Then work with your partner to practise the dialogue below. Note: both partners should talk without stopping, so the other person has to (politely) interrupt!**

A

Answer phone.

Respond. Ask the reason for B's call.

Make a suggestion.

Explain why B's suggestion isn't OK. Make another suggestion.

B

Say hello and give your name.

Explain what you need to discuss.

Explain why A's suggestion isn't OK. Make another suggestion.

Agree to A's suggestion.

8 Match the two parts of the phrases to make expressions that are commonly used when negotiating.

1	to follow	a	figure
2	room	b	schedule
3	a tight	c	a quotation
4	to meet	d	of my head
5	time	e	to say
6	that	f	a deadline
7	that's difficult	g	up our conversation
8	a ballpark	h	to manoeuvre
9	off the top	i	frame
10	to prepare	j	depends

9 Now complete the mini-dialogues using the phrases above. You may need to change the form of the expressions slightly.

A   Hello Fred. What can I do for you?

B   I'm actually calling to _____ [1] from yesterday.

A   Why do you want to change the delivery date?

B   We have a very _____ [2] on this project. If we don't get the goods by next week, we won't _____ [3] we agreed with our customer.

A   Would you be prepared to pay more for higher quality?

B   _____ [4]. I would need to talk to my boss about that.

A   What sort of _____ [5] were you thinking about for the project? I mean, when would you need our services exactly?

B   _____ [6] at the moment. We haven't made any decisions yet.

A   I can't say exactly how much it would cost.

B   Well, can you give me a _____ [7]?

A   Sorry, I would need to check the spreadsheet. I can't give you an answer _____ [8].

A   Well, I'm pleased that we managed to reach an agreement.

B   Me too. So, I'll _____ [9] and send it to you by email later today.

A   Can you give us a discount?

B   I'm afraid we don't have much _____ [10] on price.

10 Work with a partner to make a phone call. Look at the Useful Phrases below before you read your role card in the Partner Files.

PARTNER FILES ➤ Partner A   File 08, p. 49
Partner B   File 08, p. 51

USEFUL PHRASES

Making proposals	**Reacting to proposals**
I wanted to ask if there was any possibility of ...	That sounds like it would be feasible.
Would you be prepared to ...?	That sounds reasonable.
What if we ...?	That depends.
	I don't think that would be possible.

---

11 Put these sentences from the unit into the right order.

1 you I pleased if could would with work be we.

2 reasonable that sounds.

3 know head I don't off top the my of.

4 second a can interrupt I there for you?

5 meet can deadline we the?

OUTPUT

Look at what these people say about negotiating over the telephone. Which opinion(s) do you agree with?

With some of my business contacts, I only speak to them on the telephone – we never meet face to face. That makes it more of a challenge when you need to reach agreements on things. That's one reason why I always try to make small talk before we discuss business. I find small talk helps to build a personal relationship and makes discussions easier.

I find it easier to discuss things face to face than on the telephone. You can't see the other person, so it's difficult to know exactly what they are thinking. There's no body language to help you and if the other person is silent it can mean different things. Maybe they are angry with you, or maybe they are just thinking about what you have said. It's difficult to tell.

Before I make a phone call where I have to negotiate something, I think about what I want exactly. What is the minimum I am prepared to accept? What is my best alternative if we don't manage to reach an agreement? That way I know before I begin how much room to manoeuvre I have.

I don't enjoy trying to reach agreements on the telephone. I find it difficult to say no to people and to stand up for what I want. Often I hang up the phone and am not happy with the agreement I've made, but then it's too late to change anything.

OVER TO YOU

What are your strategies for reaching agreements on the telephone?

How is discussing business on the telephone different from meeting face to face, in your opinion?

What could you personally do to improve your telephone negotiating skills?

Test yourself!

See how much you've learned about telephoning in English.
Use the clues to complete the crossword puzzle.

Across

6   What's the preposition? *How ... Wednesday morning?*
7   (3 words): *Can you give me your number again, ... ?*
8   What's the preposition? *I'm tied ... all day.*
10 LSEPL: *Would you like me to ... that for you?*
13 NOSUD: *How does that ... ?*
14 Another word for *phoning*: *My name is John Ellis. I'm ... from Retex Plc.*
15 EMKA RUSE (2 words): *I'll ... she gets your message.*
19 An old way of saying *voicemail* (2 words): *I left a message on your ... .*
23 Another word for *said*: *Jonathan ... that he was going to the trade fair.*
28 LEES: *Just let me know if there's anything ... I can do for you.*
29 What's the preposition? *I have a question ... your products.*
31 What's the preposition? *Let me read that ... to you.*
32 LGUYRNTE: *We need the parts very ... .*
33 Another word for *busy*: *I'm afraid Fred's line is ... .*
34 Another word for *understand*: *Sorry, I didn't ... that.*

Down

1   LPBLRKAA GRIFUE (2 words): *Can you give me a ... ?*
2   A way to apologize: *I'll personally make sure it doesn't ... again.*
3   LACLTUYA: *I ... wanted to speak to Maria.*
4   The opposite of *postpone* (2 words): *Unfortunately my client had to ... our meeting.*
5   TUSI: *When would ... you?*
9   *Sorry, I'm not here at the moment. Please leave a ... after the tone.*
10 HDOLUS: *I think that ... be possible.*
11 XNNESETOI: *Shall I give you her ... number?*
12 TAWNED: *I ... to ask you if you have time to meet.*
16 PETCAAPIRE: *I ... your help.*
17 Another word for *seems*: *There ... to be a mistake on the invoice you sent us.*
18 *Monday at 3? Let me just check my ... .*
20 NWGOR: *I think you have the ... number.*
21 A possible answer to this question: *How are you? – Can't ... .*
22 TULNI: *I'll be in the office ... about 5 p.m. today.*
24 Another word for *pleased*: *I'm ... to hear that.*
25 RPIRNTUET: *Sorry, can I ... you there?*
26 What's the preposition? *Shall I put you ... to her?*
27 GASHTRIT: *I'll talk to my boss and then I'll call you ... back.*
28 TAXYECL: *What's the problem ... ?*
30 What's the preposition? *It's about our meeting. Something has come ... .*

Partner A   Partner Files

Unit 1, Exercise 11   File 01

Call 1

Your name is Christine/Chris Fraser. It's 10 o'clock: time to make your phone calls. (You have a meeting from 12 until 5 p.m.) Your first call is to NeuBau GmbH. You want to speak to your business contact there, Tanja Steinmann. You often call the company, so you have spoken to Tanja's PA (personal assistant) Alex several times before.

Call 2

Your name is Antoine/Antoinette Lecamus. You work for Bouret-Bouget as a secretary. Answer the phone and help the caller. Important: your boss, Yves Martignac, has told you that he doesn't want any phone calls today.

Unit 2, Exercise 7   File 02

First spell the place names below (1–4) for your partner. (The words in brackets tells you where you can find these places – they do exist!)

1 Ambato Finandrahana (Madagascar)
2 Narvskoye Vodokhranilishche (Estonia)
3 Thabana-Ntlenyana (Lesotho)
4 Lubuklinggau (Indonesia)

Then write down the words your partner spells for you (5–8).

5 _____
6 _____
7 _____
8 _____

Finally, spell the words 5–8 back to your partner to check your spelling. Did you get it right?

Unit 2, Exercise 10   File 03

Call 1

You work for RFM Electronics. Someone will call and ask about prices and telephone numbers. Look at these extracts from your current price list and internal telephone list and give them the information they need. (The price list is also available on your website www.rfm-electronics.com.)

6M138 Optocoupler	£0.70
6N148 Optocoupler	£0.90
UGN3505W Magnetic Sensor	£4.00
74AC695 Transceiver	£1.30
75AC965 Transceiver	£1.85
TD2002V Audio Amplifier	£5.40
PIC-101SCL IR Receiver Module	£3.00
Potentiometer Thumbwheel 20K	£1.45

Marketing department	+44 193 221 6760 40
Production department	+44 193 221 6760 50
Quality department	+44 193 221 6760 60
Customer service department	+44 193 221 6760 70
Purchasing department	+44 193 221 6760 80

Call 2

You work for BrightFuture Pharmaceuticals. You have received an order from NDL Inc. but you don't have a delivery address. Call NDL Inc. to get the information. You would also like the email address and mobile phone number of the person who placed the order in case you have any more questions.

Unit 3, Exercise 4   File 04

Call 1

You are Monica Thompson's voicemail! Prepare a message saying that you are not here and asking the caller to leave a message after the beep. Read it out to the caller. Then listen and make a note of the caller's message.

Call 2

You are Monica Thompson. Phone the caller back and leave a message on his voicemail, thanking him for his help. You are also interested in talking to him about a new project – ask him if he can call you back some time this week.

Unit 3, Exercise 10 — File 05

Call 1
Your name is Jay/Jill Thurber and you work for Soncha Engineering. Your colleague Gina Wilson is out of the office at the moment. Someone will call and ask for her. Take a message, checking all the details to make sure you understand them.

Call 2
Your name is Delmar/Dagmar Wagner and you work for HSF Banking Services. Your customer Sal Larkin from Bernes Insurance left a message for you, asking if you could meet him next week to talk about his company's investments. Call him and arrange a meeting. (You are free all day on Monday and Wednesday, and on Thursday morning.) Here is your business card with your phone numbers in case you have to leave a message.

HSF Banking Services
Key Account Manager
Tel (office): 0044 20 3489 2142
Tel (mobile): 0044 79 234 8234
Email: d.wagner@hsf-banking.co.uk

Unit 4, Exercise 13 — File 06

Each box represents one hour – the yellow boxes are when you are busy. Write appointments in the yellow boxes. Think of appointments which are realistic for you, for example a meeting with a client, a sales presentation, dinner with a business partner. Then role-play the three telephone conversations with your partner.

	Monday	Tuesday	Wednesday	Thursday	Friday
9 am					
10 am					
11 am					
12 noon					
1 pm					
2 pm					
3 pm					
4 pm					

Call 1
You want to meet your partner next week. You need at least two hours for the meeting. Call your partner and find a time when you are both free. (Remember that you are busy at the times marked by the yellow boxes.)

Call 2
Your partner will call you about the appointment.

Call 3
Your last meeting went on longer than you expected, and you are going to be late for your appointment with your partner. Call him/her on your mobile phone and let him/her know.

Unit 5, Exercise 10 — File 07

Call 1
While you were on a business trip to the UK last week you hired a rental car from Easy Auto. You have just received the bill and found a mistake. Call Easy Auto and complain.

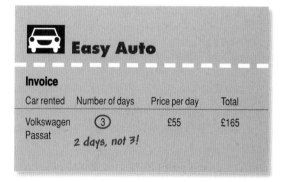

Easy Auto

Invoice

Car rented	Number of days	Price per day	Total
Volkswagen Passat	3 *2 days, not 3!*	£55	£165

Call 2
You work for a British translation agency called TransFast. A customer will call you to make a complaint. Deal with the complaint as politely and efficiently as you can. Note: you are only responsible for English/French translations, so problems with other languages are not your fault!

Unit 6, Exercise 10 — File 08

You work for the Czech subsidiary of Gilee and Soare, an American multi-national accounting firm. You are currently in charge of a three-person team which is doing an audit on a large Czech company. However the work is taking longer than you expected and you think you will need one more person on the team if you are going to meet the deadline for the work. It is time for your weekly telephone conversation with your American boss. Explain the problem to him/her and try to negotiate a solution.

Partner B   Partner Files

Unit 1, Exercise 11   File 01

Call 1

Your name is Alex Schmidt. You work for NeuBau GmbH as Tanja Steinmann's PA (personal assistant). It's ten o'clock when the phone rings. Answer the phone and help the caller. (Tanja is in a meeting until 12.30, but she is free for the rest of the day.)

Call 2

Your name is Frank/Fran Sharp. You work for Gieser Insurance Ltd. Call Bouret-Bouget and ask to speak to the CEO, Yves Martignac. You don't know him, but you want to sell him some insurance. Try as hard as you can to speak to him – don't listen to the secretary's excuses! Important: don't say why you are calling. If you say you want to sell insurance, the secretary won't let you talk to the boss.

Unit 2, Exercise 7   File 02

First write down the words your partner spells for you (1–4).

1 _____

2 _____

3 _____

4 _____

Did you get it right? Spell the words 1–4 back to your partner to check your spelling.

Finally, spell the place names below (5–8) for your partner. (The words in brackets tells you where you can find these places – they do exist!)

5 Xinjiang Uygur Zizhiqu (China)
6 Vyerkhnyadzvinsk (Belarus)
7 Romorantin-Lanthenay (France)
8 Mariscal Estigarribia (Paraguay)

Unit 2, Exercise 10   File 03

Call 1

You would like to buy some electronic components. Call RFM Electronics and ask about their prices. (Perhaps they can also send you a price list.) You also have a problem with a component you bought from RFM last month – ask for the telephone number of the customer service department.

> TD2002V Audio Amplifier
> UGN3505W Magnetic Sensor
> 6M138 Optocoupler
> 75AC965 Transceiver

Call 2

You work for NDL Inc. Two days ago you placed an order with BrightFuture Pharmaceuticals. Someone from BrightFuture will call and ask about an address. Your business address is:

    1207 Huntington Avenue, Suite 142
    San Francisco, CA 94090

The address for deliveries is:

    1209 Huntington Avenue
    San Francisco, CA 94090

Your email address is:
purchasing@ndl-corporation.com
Your cell phone number: +1 (202) 841-4588.

Unit 3, Exercise 4   File 04

Call 1

Your name is Hubert Adamczyk. You are going to phone your client Monica Thompson from Prackles Ltd. Unfortunately she is not in the office so you will have to leave a message on her voicemail. Plan what you are going to say, then call her and leave the message. Here is the information you need.

> Hi,
> I'm afraid there is a problem with the invoice you sent us last week. The total seems to be incorrect. Could you check this and get back to me?
>
> Thanks,
> Monica

> I checked the invoice – there's a mistake in it.
> Can you phone her back and tell her we'll send her a new invoice asap? Thanks!
> Rachel
>
> PS Don't forget to apologize for our mistake!

Call 2

You are Hubert Adamczyk. You will be in and out of the office for the next three days. Prepare a greeting for your voicemail service, saying when you will be available. Read it out to the caller. Then listen and make a note of the caller's message.

Unit 3, Exercise 10   File 05

Call 1

Your name is Alessandro/Alessandra Vieri and you work for Advanta Architeturra, an architect's office. Your business partner Gina Wilson from Soncha Engineering sent you an email but forgot to include the attachment. It's an important document and you need it by tomorrow. Call Gina and ask her to send you the document again.

Call 2

Your name is Rosanna/Ross Wall and you work for Bernes Insurance. Your colleague Sal Larkin is out of the office at the moment. Someone will call and leave a message for him. Write down the message, checking all the details to make sure you understand them. Make sure you get the person's office phone number and mobile number.

Unit 4, Exercise 13   File 06

Each box represents one hour – the yellow boxes are when you are busy. Write appointments in the yellow boxes. Think of appointments which are realistic for you, for example a meeting with a client, a sales presentation, dinner with a business partner. Then role-play the three telephone conversations with your partner.

	Monday	Tuesday	Wednesday	Thursday	Friday
9 am					
10 am					
11 am					
12 noon					
1 pm					
2 pm					
3 pm					
4 pm					

Call 1

Your partner wants to meet you next week. He/She will call you to arrange a time to meet. (Remember that you are busy at the times marked by the yellow boxes.)

Call 2

Something has come up and you need to change the time of the appointment with your partner. Call him/her, explain why you need to change the appointment, and find a new time.

Call 3

Your partner will call you about the meeting. He/She is talking on a mobile phone and the connection is not very good. You will need to ask him/her to repeat some things.

Unit 5, Exercise 10   File 07

Call 1

You work for a car rental company called Easy Auto. A customer will call you to make a complaint. Deal with the complaint as politely and efficiently as you can. Note: you were on holiday last week, so any mistakes made then were not your fault!

Call 2

You work for Klupp, a German engineering company. TransFast, a British translation agency, recently translated your website into English. However your boss has found some mistakes in the translation. Call TransFast and complain.

Here are some of the mistakes I've found on the website:
- *'Kühlrohr' is 'cooling pipe', not 'cool tube'*
- *'Stahlseil' is 'steel cable', not 'steel rope'*
- *'Beton' is 'concrete', not 'cement'(!)*

There were other mistakes too, but these are enough to use as examples. Can you call them and tell them about the mistakes? Make sure you find out what they'll do to solve the problem. Thanks!

Unit 6, Exercise 10   File 08

You work for Gilee and Soare, an American multi-national accounting firm. It is time for your weekly telephone conversation with your Czech subsidiary. Your contact person (who reports directly to you) is currently head of a three-person team which is doing an audit on a large Czech company. The project is already over budget. Ask for a status report on the project, and find out what your contact person is going to do to solve the problems on the project.

Answer key

UNIT 1

page 5

1

	Call 1	Call 2	Call 3
Who is calling?	John Ellis	Karen Miller	Bob
Who does he/she want to speak to?	Jörg Seide	Maria	Jörg Seide
Does he/she get through? If not, why not?	No. Jörg is in a meeting.	No. Maria's line is engaged.	Yes. But he is on the other line.
What will happen next?	Jörg will call back.	Karen will try again.	Jörg will call Bob back.

page 6

2
1 speaking
2 tell, called
3 here
4 wanted
5 hang, connection
6 afraid, engaged
7 calling
8 get
9 hear
10 line

a 1, 3   b 9   c 4   d 5   e 6, 10   f 7   g 2, 8

3

		Answer
1	Could I speak to Jörg Seide, please?	a, h
2	Can I take a message?	j
3	Could you ask him to call me back?	a, c
4	Could you tell me your name again?	d
5	Does Mr Seide have your number?	b
6	Is she there at the moment?	g
7	Shall I put you through to her?	f, j
8	Can I just ask what it's about?	i
9	Can I call you back in ten minutes?	a, c
10	Have you got my mobile number?	e

page 7

4

MORE FORMAL	LESS FORMAL
Could you please hold?	Hang on a moment.
Can I just ask what it's about?	What's it about?
Thank you.	Thanks.
Certainly.	Sure.
Shall I put you through to her?	Do you want to speak to her?

5 1 b   2 c   3 (not used on the telephone)   4 a

6 In call 1, Sylvia says Mr Ellis because the caller has a higher status than her, and also because she doesn't know him. However he calls her Sylvia because she has a lower status than him.
In call 2, Sylvia and Karen know each other (even if only from speaking on the phone) and so they use first names with each other, although Karen probably has a higher status than Sylvia.
In call 3, Jürgen and Bob use first names with each other because they know each other. It's also a sign of a close working relationship.

page 8

7 (model answers)
2 No, I'm actually from Belgium.
3 I'm afraid he's not here.

4 Actually, I'll call back later.
5 I'm afraid I won't be in the office tomorrow. / Actually, I won't be in the office tomorrow.
6 I'm afraid Heather's line is engaged. / Heather's line is actually engaged.

8 (model answers)
2 I'm afraid she's having lunch at the moment.
3 I'm sorry, but she's actually on another line.
4 I'm afraid she's out of the office today.
5 I'm sorry, but she's in a meeting at the moment.

page 9

9 (model answer)
A Kroste International. Raymond Pitt speaking.
B Hi Raymond. It's Patrick here. How are you? Did you have a good holiday in New York?
A It was really great, thanks. But I feel I need another holiday to recover!
B I can imagine. Listen Raymond, I actually wanted to talk to Lorraine. Is she there at the moment?
A I'm afraid she's not. She had to leave early today. Would you like to leave a message for her?
B Yes please. Could you ask her to call me back tomorrow morning?
A I'll do that. Well, thanks for calling Patrick. Bye now.

10 a 3   b 1   c 2   d 8   e 4   f 7   g 5   h 6

1 catch
2 could
3 up
4 wrong
5 line
6 cut
7 spell
8 slowly

page 10

12

across	down
1 CALL BACK	1 CONNECTION
4 EXTENSION	2 CALLING
5 MOBILE	3 MESSAGE
7 PUT THROUGH	6 SPEAKING
10 AFRAID	8 HOLD
11 ENGAGED	9 CATCH

The mystery word is TELEPHONE.

page 11

13 1 Kyoko Ito speaking.
2 This is Juan Suarez. Can I speak to Ms Sanders, please?
3 I'll call back later.
4 Brenda isn't in the office today.
5 Do you have my mobile number?
6 I'm afraid Mr Chang isn't in the office today.
7 I'll tell him that you called.

UNIT 2

page 12

Starter
1 a six hundred and forty-seven
b nine thousand two hundred and thirty-five
c one million, five hundred and seventy-four thousand, three hundred and eighty-nine

d one point nine five five
e fifteen euros (and) forty (cents)
f oh oh (or: zero zero) four nine, three oh (or: zero), two nine seven oh (or: zero), double six (or: six six) three four

2 A comma shows the thousand position in a number. A point shows the decimal place.

3 a underscore
b at
c hyphen (or: dash)
d dot
e (forward) slash
f back slash
g hash sign / pound sign (chiefly Am Eng) / number (The first two terms are frequently used for pre-paid phone cards and multi-choice automated phone services.)
h asterisk
i open bracket
j close bracket

1
relay switch
model RS ~~788 877~~
unit price:
1000 units = €1.~~65~~ 1.56
2000 units = €11.~~39~~ 1.49

Misha Oberemok
delivery address
~~Mitscovitch Ulittsa 6~~ Mitskevich Ulitsa
~~41000 Kiev~~ 79000
Fax no. (+380 44)
244 ~~4240~~ 42 04

page 13

2 Call 1
1 about 3 was 5 right
2 right 4 tell 6 catch

Call 2
1 calling 3 pen 5 read
2 check 4 spell 6 again

3 (model answers)
2 Could you tell me your name?
3 I just wanted to check the address.
4 What was your name again?
5 What did you want to know?
6 Could you tell me what your charge for delivery would be?
7 Could you tell me how long it would take to send it?
8 I just wanted to ask if you have time to meet tomorrow.

page 14

4
1 To Poland? 4 Let me just read that back to you.
2 Did you say 5 And your name was
3 Sorry, was that 6 So that's

page 15

5 (model answers)
2 Sorry, did you say 98 King Street?
3 Let me just read that back to you. Your number is 091 210 3885.
4 Thursday, right.
5 Prentice, right.
6 Sorry, did you say €72.90 or €72.19?

6

1	2	3	4	5	6	7
A	B	F	I	O	Q	R
H	C	L	Y		U	
J	D	M			W	
K	E	N				
	G	S				
	P	X				
	T	Z (Br Eng)				
	V					
	Z (Am Eng)					

page 16

8 3 Kevin dot Stevens at A F G hyphen* consulting dot C A
4 Margaret underscore Peterson at zebra dot I T
5 w w w dot rent hyphen* a hyphen* car dot com
(* dash also possible)

9
1 Do you have a pen? H
2 Let me just read that back to you. F
3 I'm calling about the order you faxed us yesterday. A
4 Are you the right person to ask? B
5 What would you like to know? C (G)
6 Let me just check that. J
7 Would you like me to spell that for you? I
8 What was your question? G (C)
9 Can I check that and get back to you? D
10 Can you just give me your phone number? E

page 17

11 1 Do you have a pen?
2 The order number is A for apple, E for elephant, V for Venice, zero two six.
3 Was that D for David or B for Bob?
4 His email address is Tom hyphen (or: dash) Baker at Martins dot D E.
5 Sorry, I didn't catch that. Did you say thirteen or thirty?

UNIT 3

page 19

1 (model answers)
For Valeria Giuliani / From Walter Jackson
Please call and confirm date and time for project meeting.
The 10th is OK for him. Tel: 032 345 8395

For Toshiki Kitano / From Seth Prescott
He's doing a sales presentation for a prospective client (on Friday at 9 or 10 am for 2 hours) and wants to meet with you (??) about the 'technical stuff'. He didn't leave a number.

The second message is confusing because it is poorly structured, Seth contradicts himself, he hasn't checked his facts, and he takes too long to give the message.

page 20

2
1 reached 5 beep 9 confirmed
2 Unfortunately 6 This 10 again
3 available 7 calling 11 case
4 leave 8 get 12 soon

3 (model answers)
Hi. This is Valeria Giuliani calling for Walter Jackson. Walter, I just wanted to confirm that the project meeting will take place on the 10th, starting at 9 a.m. I'm looking forward to seeing you then. Bye now.

Hello. This is Seth Prescott calling for Toshiki Kitano. I have a sales presentation next Friday for a prospective client, and I wanted to ask you if you could talk about the technical aspects. It's scheduled for 10 a.m. and it will probably last about two hours. Maybe you can call me back today to let me know if you can do it. My number is 9083 5209. Thanks a lot. Bye.

page 21

5 a call 2   b call 1   c call 2   d call 2   e call 1

(messages – model answers)
Call 1
Jonathan, Ricardo Fonseca from Aresto called about the EuroMedical fair next week. He wanted to know if you're going and if you and he can meet. Please call him back. He'll be in the office until 5 p.m. today.
Call 2
Elaine Sloan called about the team for the new marketing campaign. She wanted to know if Henry can still be on the team if they shift the deadline back a week. Call back today on 44 141 223 4569.

6 1 I'm afraid Jonathan isn't here at the moment.
2 Would you like to leave a message for him?
3 Let me get a pen.
4 Shall I ask Jonathan to call you back?
5 Does he have your number?
6 I'll make sure Jonathan gets your message.

a ... the email you sent me yesterday.
b ... Henry was too busy to join the team.
c ... that we could take Maria instead.
d ... as soon as I've had the chance to speak to him?
e ... just in case?
f ... call you straight back.

page 22

7 (model answers)
2 She told me that maybe we could find another supplier.
3 He said it would be difficult to schedule a new meeting.
4 They asked if we could deliver earlier.
5 You mentioned that you had hired two new employees.
6 He told me that he was going to the UK in June.

8 1 at   4 about
2 after, on   5 to
3 for   6 in, until

page 23

9 b Can you please give me your number again just in case?   5
c Could you get back to me on this asap, please?   8
d Would you like to leave a message for her?   3
e I'm afraid she isn't here at the moment.   6
f I'm calling about the email you sent me yesterday. 7
g I'll make sure she gets your message.   4
h I think you have my number already.   2

page 25

11 1 You can reach me on 544 332 64.
2 Would you like to leave a message for her?
3 Eileen asked me to call her back.
4 This is Mary Lamb. I'm calling about the meeting.
5 He told me that he had already sent the letter.

UNIT 4

page 26

Starter
1 b, c, and e are not possible.
2 a half (past) six or six thirty
b quarter past ten or ten fifteen
c quarter to four or three forty five
d midnight
e midday/noon
3 a January 2, 2006
b 1 February 2006
4 b, d, and e are not possible.

1 Simon makes an appointment with Alexa to meet at 10 a.m. on Wednesday in his office.

page 27

2 SUGGESTING A MEETING OR AN APPOINTMENT
(* phrases from part 2)
Could we schedule a meeting for next month?*
Do you have time to meet tomorrow?*

ASKING ABOUT OR SUGGESTING A TIME TO MEET
When would suit you?
Would that be OK for you?
We could meet in the evening ...
Well, how about Wednesday morning?
Shall we say 10 o'clock in my office?
What about Thursday?*
Where would be the best place to meet?*

SAYING IF A TIME IS CONVENIENT OR NOT
I think that should be possible.
I should be free on Tuesday morning, though.
Tuesday's bad for me, I'm afraid.
I'm tied up all day.
Sorry, I'm booked up that evening too.
Yes, that would be good for me.
Yes, I'm free then.*

CONFIRMING AN ARRANGEMENT
I'll see you on Wednesday, then.
OK, so that's 2 pm in the conference room.*

3 (model answer)
A Gina Kilshaw.
B Hi Gina. It's René here. I was wondering if you might have time to meet tomorrow, maybe at 10 am?
A Sorry, I'm tied up all morning. What about in the afternoon?
B Sorry, I'm booked up in the afternoon. How about Friday at 10?
A Yes, that would be good for me. Shall we meet in my office?
B Sounds good. So that's Friday at 10 a.m. in your office.
A Great. See you then.

page 28

4 2 is/'s flying   4 is/'s having   6 is/'s meeting
    3 is/'s meeting   5 is/'s having   7 is/'s coming

page 29

5 3 in   8 on   13 in
    4 on   9 at (BE) / on (AE)   14 in
    5 Ø   10 at (BE) / on (AE)   15 in
    6 Ø   11 at
    7 Ø   12 at

6 1 g   2 c   3 e   4 b   5 a   6 d   7 f

page 30

7 (model answer)
    A Hello. Jason Moore speaking.
    B Hi Jason. It's Petra Klein here.
    A Petra! How nice to hear from you. How are things in Cologne?
    B Pretty busy, as usual. How's the weather in England?
    A Terrible! What's it like with you?
    B Not so bad. We had a bit of sun today. So, Jason, I actually wanted to ask you about the figures you sent me …

8 The following sentences are in the dialogue: 1, 4, 5, 8

(model answer)
Simon – Alexa Johnston called. She asked if she could change the time of her meeting with you tomorrow. I changed it to 9 o'clock. Hope that's okay.

page 31

9 1 wondering, changed   4 bit, postponed
    2 wanted, missed   5 possible, delayed
    3 possibly, lasted

10 She's still waiting for the train and wants to tell Simon that she might be a few minutes late.

    1 waiting   4 catch   7 delays
    2 might   5 see   8 losing
    3 breaking 6 latest   9 better

11 1 c, d, h   2 d, e, g   3 d, e, g   4 a   5 b, f   6 f

page 32

12 1 date   4 bring forward   7 postpone
    2 cancel   5 arrangements 8 arrange
    3 appointment 6 date

14 1 I'm afraid something has come up.
    2 She has an appointment with the MD.
    3 I might be a few minutes late.
    4 I'm flying to New York on Saturday.
    5 I'm tied up all day.
    6 I should be free on Wednesday afternoon.

Output
    1 B   2 D   3 C   4 A
    1 useful, contact   3 invention, phone calls
    2 voicemail, message 4 appointment, know

UNIT 5

page 34

1 a 2   b 4   c 1   d 3
    A 1   B 2   C 4   D 3   E 2   F 4   G 1   H 3

page 35

2 There's a problem with the latest consignment: some of the boxes contain the wrong sensor model (the FR 388 instead of the FR 346). To solve the problem, Reva will send Abby 130 units of the FR 346 by express delivery with Swift Logistics.

    1 consignment   4 FR 346   7 Swift
    2 boxes   5 FR 388   8 pick
    3 sensor   6 express

3 1 appears   4 get   7 mix-up
    2 sorry   5 this   8 personally
    3 exactly   6 sorting

    describe a problem   1
    clarify what the problem is   3
    apologize   2, 7
    say how you will solve the problem 4, 5

page 36

4 (model answers)
    2 Unfortunately you delivered the consignment to the wrong address.
    3 The total on the bill appears to be wrong.
    4 I'm afraid we have a slight problem with the equipment you sold us.
    5 You seem to have sent us the wrong model.
    6 Unfortunately you gave us the incorrect information.

page 37

5 1 There appears to be a mistake
    2 Could you tell me
    3 Please accept my apologies
    4 I'll make sure that gets sorted out
    5 It seems you sent us
    6 I'm really sorry about
    7 sorry again about the mix-up

Conversation 1 is more formal; conversation 2 is more informal.

6 2 'll have   4 'll give
    3 'll personally make sure 5 'll deliver

page 38

7 (model answer)
    A I'm afraid there seems to be a small problem with your delivery dates.
    B Oh dear. Can you explain what the problem is exactly?
    A Well, in our discussions you said you could deliver by the end of September. But in the contract you sent me, it says delivery will be in the middle of October.
    B Sorry, that's entirely my fault. I forgot we had agreed on September. I'll change the contract and send you the new version.
    A Thanks.
    B No problem. And sorry again for that mistake. Bye now.

8 1 Michel
2 Euromarché
3 Receipts come out blank when printed
4 New ink cartridge sent to customer

9 1 right   3 details   5 questions, call
2 detail   4 case   6 any

page 39

11 1 There appears to be a small problem with the invoice.
2 That must be really annoying.
3 You should have the consignment first thing tomorrow.
4 Thanks for sorting that out.
5 I'll make sure it doesn't happen again.

UNIT 6

page 40

1 1 A & M   5 five
2 processor   6 ten
3 middle   7 quotation
4 shift work

page 41

2 1 d   2 a   3 f   4 b   5 c   6 e

3 4 would cost   9 gave
5 would/could cause   10 asked
6 reduced   11 could rent
7 would/could cause   12 could work
8 would be

page 42

4 (model answers)
2 We might be able to deliver by the end of the week.
3 I would say that we can solve the problem.
4 It will probably be difficult.
5 (I think) I can provisionally say that we can change the specifications of the product.

5 1 Davis   4 discount
2 price   5 five per cent
3 ten per cent   6 500

page 43

6 1 follow up   4 may be true
2 didn't you   5 something
3 interrupt

7 (model answer)
A Sandra Caspers.
B Hi Sandra. It's Rainer Thide here.
A Oh, hi Rainer. What can I do for you?
B I'm calling about the prices you quoted us for software development costs. They seem a bit too high for me. Is there any possibility of making a better price?
A Well, we could reduce the price a little if you changed your operating system to Linux. You know how it's free and it's also cheaper to …

B Sorry, can I interrupt you there? All our computers run on Windows, and there's no possibility of changing at the moment. But what about if you simplified the specification? I mean, there seems to be …
A Can I just say something? The specification we gave you is the absolute minimum. We can't simplify it. But we might be able to outsource some of the work to our partners in India. That would be cheaper.
B That sounds like it might work. Yes, maybe we can do that.

page 44

8 1 g   5 i   9 d
2 h   6 j   10 c
3 b   7 e
4 f   8 a

9 1 follow up our conversation
2 tight schedule
3 meet the deadline
4 That depends
5 time frame
6 That's difficult to say
7 ballpark figure
8 off the top of my head
9 prepare a quotation
10 room to manoeuvre

page 45

11 1 I would be pleased if we could work with you.
2 That sounds reasonable.
3 I don't know off the top of my head.
4 Can I interrupt you there for a second?
5 Can we meet the deadline?

page 46

Across	Down
6 about	1 ballpark figure
7 just in case	2 happen
8 up	3 actually
10 spell	4 bring forward
13 sound	5 suit
14 calling	9 message
15 make sure	10 should
19 answering machine	11 extension
23 mentioned	12 wanted
28 else	16 appreciate
29 about	17 appears
31 back	18 diary
32 urgently	20 wrong
33 engaged	21 complain
34 catch	22 until
	24 delighted
	25 interrupt
	26 through
	27 straight
	28 exactly
	30 up

Transcripts

Call 1

2
Sylvia	Micah Information Systems. Sylvia speaking.
John	Hello. This is John Ellis from Retex Plc. Could I speak to Jörg Seide, please?
Sylvia	I'm afraid Mr Seide is in a meeting. Can I take a message?
John	Yes, please. Could you ask him to call me back?
Sylvia	Certainly. Could you tell me your name again, please?
John	My name is John Ellis. And I'm calling from Retex Plc.
Sylvia	Does Mr Seide have your number?
John	Actually, I don't think he does. It's 00 44 140 397 834.
Sylvia	397 834. That's great. Okay, Mr Ellis, I'll tell Mr Seide you called.
John	Thanks very much, Sylvia.
Sylvia	You're welcome. Bye now.
John	Bye.

Call 2

3
Sylvia	Micah Information Systems. Sylvia speaking.
Karen	Hi Sylvia. It's Karen Miller here.
Sylvia	Oh, hi Karen. How are you?
Karen	Fine, thanks. And you?
Sylvia	Not so bad. A bit busy, as always.
Karen	I can imagine. Listen Sylvia, I actually wanted to speak to Maria. Is she there at the moment?
Sylvia	Yes, she is. Shall I put you through to her?
Karen	That would be great.
Sylvia	Can I just ask what it's about?
Karen	I wanted to ask her about the project meeting next week.
Sylvia	Thanks, Karen. Just hang on a moment while I make the connection. ... Sorry, Karen. I'm afraid Maria's line is engaged.
Karen	Oh, that's a pity. I'll try calling later.
Sylvia	Shall I give you her extension number?
Karen	Yes, please. Let me just get a pen. Okay.
Sylvia	It's 113.
Karen	113. Right. Thanks, Sylvia. Bye now.
Sylvia	Bye.

Call 3

4
Jörg	Seide.
Bob	Hi Jörg. It's Bob here.
Jörg	Oh, hi Bob. Nice to hear from you. How's business?
Bob	Oh, can't complain. How are things with you?
Jörg	Fine, thanks. Listen Bob, can I call you back in ten minutes? I'm actually talking to someone on the other line.
Bob	Sure, no problem. Have you got my mobile number?
Jörg	Yes, I have.
Bob	Great. Speak to you then.
Jörg	Bye.

Call 1

5
A	So, we have a meeting planned for next Monday.
B	Sorry, I didn't catch that.
A	I said, we have a meeting planned for next Monday.
B	Ah, okay.

Call 2

6
A	The serial number is KLT/9090/34.
B	Sorry, could you repeat that please?
A	Sorry, I said the serial number is KLT/9090/34.

Call 3

7
A	Yes, well, I think there could be a problem with the project schedule.
B	Sorry, can you speak up a bit, please?
A	Sorry. I said, I think there could be a problem with the project schedule.

Call 4

8
A	Petrex Plastics. Simon speaking.
B	Hi. Is Claire Brown there?
A	Sorry, I think you have the wrong number. There's no one of that name here.
B	Oh, sorry about that.
A	No problem.

Call 5

9
A	Anyway, when I arrived last night, I realized I forgot to take the contract with me.
B	Sorry, this is a really bad line. I didn't catch that.
A	I said, I forgot to take the contract. Can you send it to me by email?

Call 6

10
A	So, we should really try to find time next week for a meeting. What do you think? ... Hello? Are you there? Hmm. Hi, Chris?
B	Yes, I'm here. Sorry, we got cut off. I don't know what happened.
A	That's okay. Anyway, as I was saying ...

Call 7

11
A	And my last name is MacGilchrist.
B	Sorry, could you spell that for me, please?
A	Of course. It's M-A-C-G-I-L-C-H-R-I-S-T.

Call 8

12
A	Listen, I have a very quick question about the agenda for tomorrow's meeting. Could you tell me if the new marketing strategy is on the agenda?
B	Sorry, could you speak a little bit more slowly, please?
A	Sorry. I wanted to know if the new marketing strategy is on the agenda for tomorrow's meeting.

Call 1

13
Arno	HCE Ltd. Arno Maier speaking. How can I help you?
Neil	Hello. I have a question about your relay switches. Are you the right person to ask?
Arno	Yes, I am. What was your question?

Neil	I'm interested in the switch model RS 877, but I couldn't find a price for it on your website. Could you tell me what the unit price would be for orders over a thousand units?
Arno	Hang on a second, let me just check that in our system. That was the RS 877, right?
Neil	Yes, that's right.
Arno	OK ... The unit price for a thousand units or more would be 1 euro 56 cents. If you order two thousand units or more, then the unit price drops to ... let me see ... 1 euro 49 cents.
Neil	Sorry, I didn't catch the second price.
Arno	It's 1 euro 49 cents.
Neil	OK. Right, so that's 1 euro 56 cents for a thousand units or over, and 1 euro 49 cents for two thousand units or over.
Arno	That's right.
Neil	Great. Well, thank you very much.
Arno	You're welcome. Just let me know if there's anything else I can do for you.
Neil	I'll do that. Goodbye.
Arno	Bye.

Call 2

Misha	Dorogo Engineering. Misha Oberemok speaking.
Arno	Hi Misha. It's Arno Maier from HCE here.
Misha	Hello Arno. How are you?
Arno	Not bad, thanks. Listen Misha, I'm calling about the order you faxed us yesterday.
Misha	Uh huh.
Arno	The delivery address written on the fax isn't very clear, and I just wanted to check it.
Misha	OK. Let me just find my copy of the order. One second. OK. Do you have a pen?
Arno	Yes I do.
Misha	Right. The address is Mitskevich Ulitsa 6, 79000 Kiev. Would you like me to spell that for you?
Arno	Yes please.
Misha	OK. It's M-I-T-S-K-E-V-I-C-H, new word, U-L-I-T-S-A, number 6.
Arno	Let me just read that back to you. It's M-I-T-S-K-E-V-I-C-H, new word, U-L-I-T-S-A, number 6. Is that right?
Misha	Yes, that's right.
Arno	Sorry, what was the post code again?
Misha	79000.
Arno	79000. OK. And Kiev is spelt K-I-E-V, is that right?
Misha	Exactly.
Arno	OK. And one last thing. We don't have your fax number and the number on your fax was hard to read. What were the last four digits?
Misha	Mmm. That's 42 04.
Arno	Sorry, did you say 42 04 or 42 14?
Misha	42 04.
Arno	Great. OK, Misha, I think that was everything. I'll make sure the order gets sent off today. Thanks very much for your help.
Misha	No problem. Speak to you later.
Arno	Bye.

UNIT 3, EXERCISE 1

Message 1

15 Hello. You've reached Lessa Logistica. Unfortunately no one is available to take your call at the moment. Our normal office hours are 9 to 5, Mondays to Fridays. Please leave a message after the beep or send us a fax on 021 991 8814. Thank you.

Hello. This is Walter Jackson calling for Valeria Giuliani. Valeria, I'm calling about the planned project meeting. You asked me if the 10th would be okay for me, and I just wanted to confirm that it is. Maybe you can get back to me as soon as you've confirmed the date and time with everyone. I think you have my number already, but here it is again, just in case. It's 032 345 8395. Hope to speak to you soon. Bye.

Message 2

16 Hi. Can you help me next, um, what day is the tenth? Thursday? No, Friday. That's right, Friday. Maybe at 10 a.m.? Let me think – would that give us enough time? We could also meet at 9. That might be better actually. Oh, I almost forgot – I need you to talk about technical stuff. We'll probably need two hours. It's for a prospective client – I'm doing a sales presentation for them. Oh, this is Seth Prescott by the way. And this message is for Toshiki ... Toshiki ... er ... Kitano, that's it, Toshiki Kitano. Bye. Oh, wait a moment, I don't think you have my number. It's ...

UNIT 3, EXERCISE 5

Call 1

Anke	JKL Consulting. Anke Schmidt speaking.
Ricardo	Hello. This is Ricardo Fonseca from Aresto. Could I speak to Jonathan Leary, please?
Anke	Oh, I'm afraid Jonathan isn't here at the moment. Would you like to leave a message for him?
Ricardo	Yes, please.
Anke	Just a moment. Let me get a pen. [pause] Okay, I'm ready now. Go ahead.
Ricardo	Right. I was calling about the EuroMedical trade fair next week. Jonathan mentioned that he was thinking about going. So I just wanted to check if he'll be there, and if so, if he has time to meet me.
Anke	Let me just make sure that I got that right. You're going to the EuroMedical trade fair next week, and you'd like to know if Jonathan will be there, and if the two of you can meet.
Ricardo	That's right.
Anke	Shall I ask Jonathan to call you back?
Ricardo	Yes, that would be good.
Anke	OK. Erm ... does he have your number?
Ricardo	Yes, he does. I'll be in the office until about 5 p.m. today if he wants to call me.
Anke	That's great. I'll make sure Jonathan gets your message.
Ricardo	Thanks very much.
Anke	You're welcome. Bye for now.
Ricardo	Bye.

Call 2

18

Anke	JKL Consulting. Anke Schmidt speaking.
Elaine	Hi Anke. This is Elaine Sloan.
Anke	Oh hi, Elaine. How are you doing?
Elaine	Fine thanks, and you?
Anke	Oh, can't complain. So, what can I do for you?
Elaine	I'm calling about the email you sent me yesterday, about the team for the new marketing campaign. You said that Henry was too busy to join the team and you told me that we could take Maria instead.
Anke	That's right.
Elaine	Well, we would really like to have Henry if possible, so I wanted to make a suggestion. Do you think Henry would have time if we shifted the deadline back, say, a week or so?
Anke	Mmm, that might be possible, but I'll have to talk about it with Henry first.
Elaine	Of course.
Anke	Can I call you back later today as soon as I've had the chance to speak to him?
Elaine	Sure. I'll be here all day. You've got my number, right?
Anke	I think so, but can you give it to me again just in case?
Elaine	Yes. It's 44 for Britain, then 141 223 4569.
Anke	Let me read that back to you. 141 223 4569, is that right?
Elaine	Yes, that's right.
Anke	Great. Okay, I'll talk to Henry and call you straight back.
Elaine	Thanks Anke. Talk to you later.
Anke	Bye.

UNIT 4, EXERCISE 1

19

Simon	Simon Mellor.
Alexa	Hi Simon. It's Alexa Johnston here.
Simon	Oh, hi Alexa. How are you doing?
Alexa	Can't complain. How are things in Frankfurt?
Simon	Oh, you know what it's like. Business as usual! So, what can I do for you, Alexa?
Alexa	Well, I'm going to be in Frankfurt next week, and I was wondering if you might have time to meet me for an hour or two while I'm in town. It would give us the chance to talk about the Allianz project, among other things.
Simon	Yes, that's a good idea. Let me just think for a moment ... I think that should be possible. I just need to check my diary. Hang on a sec. (*pause*) Right. When would suit you?
Alexa	Let me think. I'm flying in on Monday morning. I'll be in a meeting all afternoon and then I'm having dinner with my client in the evening. I should be free on Tuesday morning, though. Would that be OK for you?
Simon	Tuesday's bad for me, I'm afraid. I'm tied up all day. We could meet in the evening for something to eat, though.
Alexa	Sorry, I'm booked up that evening too. Mmm, this is getting a bit difficult.
Simon	Well, how about Wednesday morning?
Alexa	Yes, that would be good for me.
Simon	Brilliant. Shall we say 10 o'clock in my office?

Alexa	Yes, that sounds good. Oh, by the way, I'll have my mobile with me if you need to get in touch. You have the number, right?
Simon	Yes, I do. OK, Alexa, I'll see you on Wednesday, then.
Alexa	Excellent. See you.
Simon	Bye.

UNIT 4, EXERCISE 4

20

Hilary	JPL Consulting. Hilary Wilkins speaking.
Anna	Hello Hilary. This is Anna Roth from Frankfurt. Is Alexa there?
Hilary	I'm afraid she isn't. Can I help at all?
Anna	Well, a colleague told me that Alexa is coming to Frankfurt next week. I'd like to see her while she's here, if she has time.
Hilary	Okay. Well, let me look at her schedule and we'll figure something out. When would suit you best?
Anna	I'm pretty flexible. Maybe you can tell me when she's free?
Hilary	Let me see. Okay, so she's flying to Frankfurt first thing on Monday morning. Then she's meeting a client at 12. In the evening she's having dinner with a friend.
Anna	Hmm. Sounds like she's quite busy. What about Tuesday?
Hilary	Well, she's free on Tuesday morning. But then she's having lunch with a colleague at 1 and she's meeting someone in the evening.
Anna	Okay. And Wednesday?
Hilary	That's pretty full. She has a couple of meetings during the day then she's coming back to London in the evening.
Anna	Okay. Well, maybe you can pencil me in on Tuesday morning. Say, 10 o'clock?
Hilary	10 o'clock on Tuesday. Okay, I'll double-check that with Alexa and send you a quick email to confirm the meeting.
Anna	Wonderful. Thanks for your help.
Hilary	You're welcome. Bye now.

UNIT 4, EXERCISE 8

21

Thorsten	Thorsten Hofmeister.
Alexa	Hello, this is Alexa Johnston. May I speak to Simon Mellor, please?
Thorsten	He's actually in a meeting at the moment. But maybe I can help you.
Alexa	Well, I'm calling about our meeting tomorrow. I'm afraid something has come up. One of my clients has brought forward our appointment in the afternoon to 12 o'clock. So I wanted to ask Simon if we could meet a bit earlier in the morning, so that I don't have to rush.
Thorsten	Let me just check Simon's schedule. OK ... How about 9 o'clock?
Alexa	Yes, that sounds fine.
Thorsten	Great. I'll tell Simon about the new time. And just give me a call if there are any more changes.
Alexa	I'll do that. Thanks very much for your help.
Thorsten	You're welcome. Bye now.

UNIT 4, EXERCISE 10

Simon	Simon Mellor.
Alexa	Hi Simon, Alexa again.
Simon	Oh, hi Alexa. What's up?
Alexa	I'm actually still waiting for the train so I'm afraid I might be a few minutes late.
Simon	Sorry, you're breaking up a little. I didn't catch that last part.
Alexa	I said I might be a few minutes late to your office.
Simon	Oh, OK. That's no problem. I'll see you when I see you.
Alexa	I should be there by 9.15 at the latest, but I'll call you again if there are any more delays. Listen, I think I'm losing the connection. I'd better go.
Simon	Sure. See you in a few minutes.
Alexa	Bye.

UNIT 4, OUTPUT

Speaker one

Mobile phones can be useful, but I don't like the fact that people can always contact me. Sometimes I just want to be left alone!

Speaker two

I wish people would be more considerate and switch their phones off when they don't need them. And I don't know why people feel they always need to answer their phone if it rings during a meeting or at the cinema. Surely they can let their voicemail pick up and then listen to any messages later.

Speaker three

I hate mobile phones! I think they're one of the most annoying inventions ever. And people make so many pointless phone calls now. Like if you're meeting someone, it used to be that you just arranged a time and then met at that time and place. Now everyone feels that they have to phone twenty times before the meeting to say that they're going to be five minutes late, or to change the time, or whatever.

Speaker four

My mobile phone has made my life much easier. Now I never need to worry about being late for an appointment; if I'm stuck in traffic, I just call and let the person know.

UNIT 5, EXERCISE 1

Extract 1

A   I'm calling from RS Plastics. There appears to be a mistake on the invoice you sent us.
B   I'm very sorry about that. Let me put you through to our accounts department. They'll sort it out for you.
A   Thanks.

Extract 2

A   Anyway, I'm actually calling about the email you sent me. You seem to have forgotten the attachment.
B   Oh dear. Sorry about that. I'll send you the file right away.
A   That would be great, thanks.

Extract 3

A   It's about the delivery we received yesterday. Some of the components don't seem to work.
B   Really? I'm very sorry about that. Can I check that and call you back?
A   Sure, no problem.

Extract 4

A   There's a problem with our network. The email server doesn't seem to be working.
B   You actually need to speak to our technical support hotline. Unfortunately I can't put you through directly, but let me give you the number.
A   That would be good, thanks.

UNIT 5, EXERCISE 2

Reva	Hume Sensors. Reva Burgos speaking.
Abby	Hello Reva, this is Abby Dickson from Sykes Electronics here.
Reva	Oh hello, Abby, how are you?
Abby	I'm a bit stressed to tell the truth. There appears to be a small problem with your latest consignment.
Reva	Oh dear. I'm sorry to hear that. What's the problem exactly?
Abby	Well, you know we ordered your FR 346 sensor last week.
Reva	Yes. 1200 units, if I remember correctly.
Abby	Exactly. Anyway, some of the boxes contain the wrong sensor model, namely the FR 388.
Reva	Oh, I'm very sorry about that. That must be really annoying.
Abby	Well, it has caused problems with our production schedule, to be honest.
Reva	Yes, I can imagine. It's good that you've brought it to my attention. Listen Abby, I'll get on to this problem immediately. How many units are missing exactly?
Abby	Let me just check … 130.
Reva	130. Right. Well, this is what I'm going to do. I'll send you 130 units of the FR 346 by express delivery with Swift Logistics. You should have them first thing tomorrow morning.
Abby	That's excellent. Shall I send you the wrong sensors back?
Reva	Yes, I'll tell the logistics company to pick the boxes up when they deliver the correct units.
Abby	Great. Well, thanks for sorting that out, Reva.
Reva	It's the least I can do. Again, I'm really sorry about the mix-up. I'll personally make sure it doesn't happen again.
Abby	That's great, Reva. Thank you. Talk to you later.
Reva	Bye for now.

UNIT 5, EXERCISE 8

Anja	Nexus Retail Systems. Technical Support Hotline. Anja speaking.
Michel	Hello. This is Michel from Euromarché. There appears to be a problem with our cash register system. Are you the right person to talk to?
Anja	I certainly am. Could you explain the problem in more detail?
Michel	Well, when we want to print receipts they come out blank.

Anja	I see. OK, I'm going to need some more details to solve the problem. First of all, when did this problem start?
Michel	Yesterday afternoon, I think.
Anja	Uh huh. And did the receipts suddenly go blank, or did it happen gradually?
Michel	It happened gradually. First the writing got lighter, and then it disappeared completely.
Anja	In that case, it must be the ink cartridge. The ink must be finished. That's easy to fix. OK, Michel, this is what I'll do. I'll send you a new ink cartridge today. You'll have it by tomorrow.
Michel	And can I install it myself?
Anja	Yes, it's very easy. The instructions are on the packaging, but if you have any questions just give me a call. My name's Anja Schneider, but you can speak to any of our operatives here on the hotline.
Michel	That's great. I'm glad it's nothing serious. Thanks for your help.
Anja	You're very welcome.
Michel	Bye now.
Anja	Bye.

UNIT 6, EXERCISE 1

🔊 33

Helen	A & M Semiconductors. Helen Tanner speaking.
Carles	Hello. This is Carles Ferran calling from K Systems in Barcelona.
Helen	Hello Mr Ferran. What can I do for you?
Carles	We're thinking about placing an order with you for processor chips.
Helen	Really? I'm pleased to hear that.
Carles	The only thing is, we need the chips very urgently. We've just won a contract with a major new customer.
Helen	Congratulations. How quickly do you need the chips exactly?
Carles	We need them by the middle of next month at the latest.
Helen	Right, so that would be in five weeks' time. I have to say that's a pretty tight schedule.
Carles	You're right, but we really need them by then if we're going to meet our project deadlines with our customer. If you weren't able to deliver by then, we would have to go to another supplier. You're our first choice however, so it would be good if we could find a way to work with you.
Helen	Of course I would like that as well. Let me think for a moment. Normally we need six to eight weeks from order to delivery. However, if we introduced shift work at the factory, then we would probably be able to manufacture the chips faster.
Carles	Well, that sounds like it would be feasible.
Helen	Yes, but shift work is more expensive. Would you be prepared to pay more for the chips in order to get them faster?
Carles	That depends. How much more expensive would they be?
Helen	That's difficult to say. I'd need to do the calculations.
Carles	Well, can you give me a ballpark figure?
Helen	Let me think. Off the top of my head, I would say between 5 to 10 per cent more expensive.

Carles	OK. Well, I'll have to check that with my boss, but I think I can provisionally say that we could work with that.
Helen	Great. So maybe you can talk to your boss and I can work out a quotation for you, and then we can talk again.
Carles	Sounds good. How quickly can you prepare the quotation?
Helen	I'll have it ready by tomorrow. I'll send it to you by email, and then we can talk again.
Carles	Great. Talk to you tomorrow, then.
Helen	Bye.

UNIT 6, EXERCISE 5

🔊 34

Francesca	Hineman Pharmaceuticals. Francesca Davis speaking.
Viktor	Hello. This is Viktor Klein calling from Swiss Optik in Basel.
Francesca	Ah, Mr Klein, nice to hear from you again.
Viktor	I'm calling because I wanted to follow up our conversation from yesterday. Remember, we talked about a possible order for saline solution.
Francesca	That's right. You said you wanted to compare products and prices from different suppliers, didn't you?
Viktor	Yes. Well I've done that now, and I'm pleased to say that we are interested in your product.
Francesca	Wonderful. Shall I fax you the order form? We could …
Viktor	Sorry, can I interrupt you there? There's actually one small problem. The price you offered us is roughly ten per cent higher than the competition, and I …
Francesca	Well yes, that may be true, but I think you'll find our quality is higher and …
Viktor	Yes, yes, but can I just say something? I wanted to ask if there was any possibility of a discount, say if we ordered a certain quantity. What do you think?
Francesca	Well, I think we have a certain amount of room to manoeuvre, but I would have to check with my boss first. Can I talk to her and get back to you?
Viktor	Certainly.
Francesca	I can do that right now if you don't mind waiting for a couple of minutes. Is that OK?
Viktor	No problem.
Francesca	Great. I'll just put you on hold. … Hello? Mr Klein?
Viktor	Yes, I'm here.
Francesca	Right, I've spoken to my boss and I can offer you a five per cent discount on orders over 500 cases. How does that sound?
Viktor	Five per cent when we order more than 500 cases? That sounds very reasonable. Of course, I'd need to discuss that again with my boss, but I think I can tentatively say that you can expect an order from us in the next couple of days.
Francesca	I'm delighted to hear that. Just let me know if there's anything else I can help you with.
Viktor	I'll do that. Anyway, I'm sure we'll talk soon.
Francesca	I'll look forward to that.
Viktor	Bye now.
Francesca	Bye.

Useful phrases and vocabulary

Opening a call

Identifying yourself
This is Leo Pearson from Griffin Plc.
It's Steve Ronson (from) AFS here.

Explaining the reason for the call
I'm calling about ...
I have a question about ...
I wanted to ask about ...
Are you the right person to ask?

Getting through to the right person

Asking for the person
Could I speak to Bob Little, please?
Is Katja there, please?
Could you put me through to your accounts
    department, please?
Listen, Steve, I'm actually trying to get through to
    Paula. Is she there at the moment?

When the person isn't available
Oh, that's a pity. I'll try calling later.
Can I leave a message for him/her?
Can you ask him/her to call me back, please?

Taking a call

Identifying yourself
Micah Information Systems. Sylvia speaking.
HCE Ltd. Arno Maier speaking. How can I help you?
So, what can I do for you?

Transferring a call
Can I just ask what it's about?
Can you hold on a moment, please?
Can you hold the line, please?
I'll put you through.
I'm connecting you now.
The line's (still) busy.
Would you like to wait, or shall I ask him/her to call
    you back?
I'm afraid his/her line is engaged (Am Eng: busy).
    Shall I give you his/her extension number?

When the other person isn't available
I'm afraid Ms Thomson is unavailable at the
    moment.
She's on another line/in a meeting/on a business
    trip.
I'm sorry, but Derek isn't in the office today.
Can I take a message?
Would you like to leave a message for her/him?
Would you like to call back later?
Can I help at all?

Calling someone back

Sorry, I'm really busy at the moment. Can I call you
    back later today/in ten minutes?
I'm actually talking to someone on the other line.
I think I've got your number, but can you give it to
    me again just in case?

Returning a call

I'm just returning your call from yesterday.
You left a message on my answering machine.

Ending the call

Thank you very much.
    → You're welcome.
Just let me know if there's anything else I can do
    for you.
    → I'll do that.
Speak to you later.
Bye now./Goodbye.

Communication problems

I didn't catch that (last part).
Could you repeat that, please?
Can you speak up a bit, please?
Could you speak a little bit more slowly, please?
Could you spell that for me, please?
This is a really bad line.
Sorry, we got cut off. ... Anyway, as I was saying, ...

Messages (in person)

Taking a message
Can I take a message?
Does (s)he have your number?
I'll tell him/her you called.
Shall I ask him/her to call you back?
I'll make sure he/she gets your message.

Checking the message
Let me just read that back to you.
Let me just make sure that I got that right.
You'd like to know if ...
Was that M for Michael or N for Nancy?
Sorry, did you say 42 04 or 42 14?
Sorry, what was the post code again?

Leaving a message
Could you ask him/her to call me back?
My name is John Ellis. I'm calling from Retex Plc and
    my number is ...

Messages (answering machines)

Greetings

You've reached Lessa Logistica.

Unfortunately no one is available to take your call at the moment.

Our normal office hours are 9 to 5, Mondays to Fridays.

Please leave a message after the beep or send us a fax on (Am Eng: at) ...

Hello. This is Cecilia's voicemail. I'm out of the office until 3 p.m./the 5th. If it's urgent, please contact Jeff on (Am Eng: at) extension 439. Thanks.

Leaving a message

This is Walter Jackson calling for Toshiki Kitano.

I'm calling about ...

Maybe you can get back to me.

I think you have my number already, but here it is again just in case. It's ...

I'll be in the office until 6 p.m. today if you want to call me.

Hope to speak to you soon.

Mobile phones

Where are you?
- → I'm on the train.
- → I'm actually in the office. You can call me on my landline.
- → I'm afraid I'm in a meeting at the moment. Can I call you later?

Have you got a couple of minutes?

My battery's low – we might get cut off, I'm afraid.

Sorry, you're breaking up (a little).

Listen, I think I'm losing the connection. I'd better go.

Small talk

Asking how someone is

How are you?

How are you doing?

How's business?

How are things in Prague?

Answers

Fine, thanks. And you?

Not (so) bad.

A bit busy, as always.

Oh, can't complain. How are things with you?

Small talk questions

What have you been up to?
- → Nothing much, apart from work, to be honest.
- → I've just got back from holiday.

How's the weather over there?
- → Wet, as usual!
- → Really nice, for a change.

How was your holiday?
- → Very nice. We had a great time.
- → Don't ask! It was a complete disaster.

Making arrangements

Suggesting a meeting

Do you have time to meet next week?

I was wondering if you might have time to meet next week.

It would give us the chance to talk about ...

Suggesting times and places

When would suit you?

Where would you like to meet?

Would Monday be OK for you?

How about Wednesday morning?

Shall we say 10 o'clock in my office?

Maybe you can pencil me in on Tuesday morning.

Reacting to suggestions

I just need to check my diary.

I think that should be possible.

Tuesday's bad for me, I'm afraid.

I'm tied up all day.

Yes, that would be good for me.

Confirming an arrangement

OK, so I'll see you Wednesday, then.

So that's Monday at 10 a.m. at your office.

Changing arrangements

I'm calling about our meeting tomorrow.

I'm afraid something has come up.

One of my clients has cancelled/brought forward our appointment.

The meeting lasted longer than I expected.

I wanted to ask you if we could meet a bit earlier/postpone our meeting.

I was wondering if we could reschedule our appointment.

Would it be possible to meet a bit later?

When you are late for an appointment

I'm afraid my meeting has taken longer than I expected.

I might be a few minutes late.

I should be there by 3 at the latest.

Complaints

Making a complaint

Are you the right person to talk to?

There appears to be a small problem with your latest consignment.

There appears to be a mistake on the invoice you sent us.

You seem to have forgotten the attachment.

Some of the components don't seem to work.

Clarifying the problem

What's the problem exactly?

Could you explain the problem in more detail?

Apologizing
I'm very/extremely sorry about that.
Please accept my apologies.
That's entirely our fault.
There must have been a mix-up.

Taking action
It's good that you've brought this problem to my
    attention.
This is what I'll do.
I'll make sure it gets sorted out straight away.
Let me put you through to our accounts
    department. They'll sort it out for you.
You actually need to speak to our technical support
    hotline. Unfortunately I can't put you through
    directly, but let me give you the number.

Ending on a positive note
Again, I'm really sorry about the mix-up.
Well, thanks for sorting that out.
    → It's the least I can do.
I'll personally make sure it doesn't happen again.
If you have any questions just give me a call.

Reaching agreements

Making proposals
I wanted to make a suggestion.
I have an idea.
What do you think?
How does that sound?

Interrupting
Sorry, can I interrupt you there?
Yes, yes, but can I just say something?
Well yes, that may be true, but...
Can I just come in here?
Can I just stop you there?

Reacting to proposals
That sounds feasible/very reasonable.
We could probably work with that.
That depends./That's difficult to say.
I don't think that would be possible.
I think we have a certain amount of room to
    manoeuvre, but I would have to check with my
    boss first.

Useful verbs (in context)

to call sb back	Can I call you back later today?
to catch	Sorry, I didn't catch your name.
to connect	I'm connecting you now.
to get cut off	Sorry, we got cut off. Where were we?
to get back to sb on sth	I'm not entirely sure. Can I get back to you on that?
to get in touch	I'm trying to get in touch with Mr Ellis.
to get through	I'm trying to get through to the sales department.
to hold	Could you please hold? I'll try to connect you.
to leave a message	Would you like to leave a message for him?
to put sb through	Shall I put you through to Mr Seide?
to reach sb on	You can reach him on his mobile.
to read sth back to sb	Let me just read that back to you.
to receive a phone call	I received a phone call from your colleague yesterday.
to return sb's call	I'm just returning your call from earlier.
to spell	Could you spell that for me please?
to speak up	Sorry, I can't hear you. Can you speak up a bit, please?
to take a message	I'm afraid he's in a meeting. Can I take a message?

British English	American English
(also) answerphone	answering machine
diary	planner
half (past) two	half past two
mobile (phone)	cell (phone)
on extension 439	at extension 439
send us a fax on 897 543	send us a fax at 543 2111
the line is engaged	the line is busy